HISTORY'S GREATEST LIBELS

By
Steve Byas

First published by Dog Ear Publishing
4011 Vincennes Rd
Indianapolis, IN 46268
www.dogearpublishing.net

ISBN: 978-1-4575-3967-1

This book is printed on acid-free paper.

Printed in the United States of America

TABLE OF CONTENTS

W e hear them almost every day, sometimes many times a day. We are bombarded with them in schools from pre-school to graduate school, on television and radio, on the Internet, in books and in magazines, and around the supper table, lunch counters, and break rooms. Lies. Lies about individuals in history, groups in history, even ideas and concepts.

The lies are told so often that they have become widely accepted, and not just by those we would place on the progressive Left, but these lies are pervasive among those who favor limited government, such as conservatives and libertarians.

I have chosen to call this book *History's Greatest Libels*, because a libel is a written communication in which the story teller *knows* it to be false, designed to damage another person's reputation, and which is successful in the destruction of the targeted person's standing in the community. Now, I will grant that the overwhelming majority of those persons repeating these lies don't actually know that they are repeating a lie, so technically speaking, it is not libel, which is actionable in court. And, of course, these lies are often spoken, so even if the person were to make a false statement which exhibits *actual malice*, it is *slander*, not libel.

But, someone at some point and time *did* know that these stories about historical figures are out and out lies, and a goodly number today either know they are lies, or have actual disregard for the truth, and repeat them anyway.

For example, almost every adult has heard the story that French Queen Marie Antoinette once said, "Let them eat cake," in response to the pleas of starving citizens of Paris during the French Revolution. The problem with the story, used to illustrate the supposed callousness of the French aristocracy and place the blame for the conflagration of the Revolution upon the Queen, is that it is completely bogus. The statement was first attributed to a French aristocrat long before Marie was even *born*. It is even unlikely that the previous attribution is even true.

Why would anyone do such a thing? What could be the possible motive for creating a false picture about an historical person, group, or incident? In the case of the libel on Marie Antoinette, it is an effort to rewrite the history of the French Revolution, which became the model for future revolutions on the Left, including the Bolshevik Revolution, which brought the horrors of communism to Russia.

When I was in high school, I drifted into the school library, and saw a book on the shelf, George Orwell's classic dystopian novel, *Nineteen Eighty-four*. In one's life, even among habitual readers, there are probably no more than a dozen books that really "stick with" the reader for a lifetime. In my case, this was one such book. Written in 1948 (Orwell is thought to have simply reversed the last two numbers to arrive at the title), is was a warning about what life could be like in the future if the trends in Orwell's time continued.

One memorable scene in the book largely answers the *purpose* behind this distortion of history. In the scene, it was said that *those who control the present control the past, and those who control the past control the future.*

Those who work so hard to distort what really happened in history, with individuals, groups, and ideas, have a desire to control the future. The past, it seems, can be used as a blunt instrument, a weapon if you will, to bludgeon modern society into submission. By distorting the past, those who repeat the greatest libels in history hope to shape the future.

This book is a modest attempt to offer an alternative to some of these libels. An alternative I call the truth.

WHAT IS LIBEL?

I t was an unusually warm day for the first Saturday in November. I was standing in front of Wright's grocery in east Norman, Oklahoma, meeting potential voters as they rushed in and out of the store. I was a candidate for state representative, and I had decided this would be "soft" campaigning, a good way to close the campaign before the Tuesday election.

I was confident of victory. The Oklahoma Republican Party had conducted a poll on my race, and five other races only two weeks earlier. According to the poll, I was 12 points ahead, with 46 percent of the vote, compared to only 34 percent for my Democrat opponent. A third-party candidate had been the choice of four percent of those polled, with 16 percent residing in the "undecided column."

My pager went off. This was 1996, and I did not yet have a cell phone. At the time, there were still an abundance of pay phones, such as the one next to me. The number on the pager was that of my good friend, Eddie Reed.

Eddie told me about a flier that he had just received, put out by my opponent's campaign. The flier asserted that Steve Byas believed the United States government had blown up the Alfred P. Murrah federal building in Oklahoma City. This was less than two years after that horrific tragedy perpetrated by Timothy McVeigh, Terry Nichols, and as the federal grand jury which indicted them put it, "others unknown." Emotions were still very raw, and the legislative district was only about 20 miles from the site of what was then the nation's worst case of terrorism on American soil.

My immediate reaction was that I could not overcome this last-minute lie. My mind began to race, considering what I could possibly do to mitigate the effects of this cold and calculated fabrication. I first tried stopping further distribution of the flier by calling my opponent. He had already been sued by his Democratic primary opponent, so I threatened a "second libel suit" if he did not halt distribution of the flier.

He refused to stop, continuing the distribution of about 5,000 copies of the libel. I crafted a response, which I took to a local copy shop, and picked up the next morning, before dawn. Despite help from several supporters in the distribution of my rebuttal, I fell 179 votes short of victory on election day. I had 47 percent of the vote—-1 point more than the poll—-while my opponent took 49 percent. The third party candidate had the same 4 percent the poll had indicated he would get. *Fifteen of the sixteen undecided points had gone to my opponent.* I had actually *won* the absentee vote, about 80 percent of which had been cast before the notorious flier.

While I had hotly threatened a libel suit, I knew its chances for success were slim. Still, I retained a lawyer, and we soon discovered that no one had ever won such a suit, at least not that we could find.

The lawsuit was filed, and almost one year later, a Cleveland County jury, by unanimous vote, found that my opponent had indeed committed libel, and I was awarded both compensatory and punitive damages. He lost on appeal, before the Court of Civil Appeals and before the Oklahoma Supreme Court.

Why had I been able to win a libel suit, despite the odds?

In the United States, it is very difficult for a "public figure" to win a libel suit, and I am glad that it is. A public figure, like an elected official, candidate, or celebrity, must prove that the person intended to damage someone's reputation, and that it was not some innocent mistaken statement, or "joke." Even proving such actual malice will not always result in any monetary damages. If one cannot prove damage, then no monetary award can be made in the case. For example, several years ago, the Baptist preacher Jerry Falwell sued a pornographic publisher. The magazine had used a cartoon in the magazine which portrayed Falwell and his mother having sexual relations in an outhouse. While one could make a case for actual malice, it is doubtful that anyone could actually believe such an incident had taken place. Thus, no damage, and no award, or very little.

I was able to prove damage because of the poll which demonstrated that almost *all* the undecided vote went to my opponent, and that I had won the absentee vote taken before the flier's distribution. Actual malice was the greater hurdle, in my case, because I had to prove to the jury that my opponent did not know that his statement was untrue. Unfortunately for him, he was unable to produce any evidence to convince the jury that he had any reason to believe such a thing.

At least I was able to use the court system to win back some of my reputation. Despite the jury's verdict, there will always be some who believe that I think the U.S. government blew up the Murrah building.

Perhaps the closing argument of my attorney illustrates this point. He told the jury of a woman who had repeated a story about a fellow church member, a story she later discovered to be false. While she apologized to the woman, she feared that there would always be some who would continue to believe the lie, the lie she had told, and had not doubt been repeated by those who heard the lie from her.

She visited her pastor, whose office overlooked a valley, He invited her to follow him outside, as he picked up a pillow off the couch. Once outside, the pastor took his pocket knife, and proceeded to rip open the pillow, causing feathers to scatter over the cliff. He shook the pillow until all the feathers were being carried by the wind and by gravity over the valley. He then turned to her, and said, "Now, go pick up all those feathers."

The woman shook her head and said, "Pastor, that is impossible. I could never retrieve all those feathers. There would always be some I could never find."

The pastor nodded. "That is the way it is when you bear false witness about another person. Once the lie is told, you can never retrieve it completely. You can never heal all the damage."

While I was able to retain an able lawyer, and successfully sue in court to regain some of my public reputation, many of the individuals and groups I discuss in this book can no longer defend themselves, either in a court of law, or even in the court of public opinion. Most are dead. Despite their demise, they do not deserve to be libeled. Others mistakenly hear these lies, repeat them, causing injustice to the dead person's reputation.

I am unable to pick up every "feather" of every lie told throughout world history. But this book is my effort to pick up a few. After you read this book, perhaps you can join me in picking up some of these lies, defending those who can no longer defend themselves.

LIBEL #1

GEORGE WASHINGTON WAS A DEIST, NOT A CHRISTIAN

As I stood at the tomb of George Washington during my trip to Mount Vernon, I was struck by the Bible verse on the wall. Taken from the Gospel of John, it is a quotation from Jesus, to reassure Martha, the sister of Jesus' dead friend, Lazarus: "I am the resurrection, and the life: he that believeth in me, though he were dead, yet shall he live."

Strange, I thought. *Strange that a deist would have at his burial plot a statement of belief in the bodily resurrection of Jesus Christ.* Since deists believe in a Creator of the universe, who otherwise does not intervene in human affairs, belief in just about *any* Christian doctrine, much less the belief in the literal physical resurrection of its Founder would be a flat contradiction.

One has to concede, I suppose, that once they but your dead body in a tomb, there is just not a whole lot you can do about others putting up any kind of saying they like. But, one has to wonder why the family of George and Martha Washington would erect a placard with such an explicitly Christian statement supporting the doctrine of the bodily resurrection of Christian believers.

Perhaps it is because George Washington was *not* a deist at all, but rather a Christian?

Contemporaries of Washington certainly believed our first president and the "father of our country" was a Christian. Jonathan Mitchell Sewall contended that Washington was a "firm believer in the Christian religion." Sewall was very aware of the deist assertion, and told an audience in New Hampshire less than one month after Washington's death, "Let the deist reflect on this, and remember that Washington, the savior of his country, did not disdain to acknowledge and adore a great Savior, whom deists and infidels affect to slight and despise" (Johnson 251-252).

John Marshall, who sat as Chief Justice of the Supreme Court for more than a quarter of a century, was a personal friend of Washington's.

Marshall wrote a biography of Washington, arguing that Washington was a "sincere believer in the Christian faith, and a truly devout man" (Johnson 260).

It must be said, of course, that while Marshall, Sewall, and many others had no doubt as to Washington's personal Christian faith, no one but God can know the heart of a human being. While the testimony of others is not conclusive, by itself, that Washington was a sincere believer in Jesus Christ as his personal Savior, the evidence appears strong that Washington did, in fact, trust his eternal destiny to faith in Christ. There is no evidence that Washington *ever* expressed deistic views. When he survived smallpox as a young man, he credited his recovery to "the miraculous care of Providence" (Gragg 17).

According to *George Washington, the Christian*, by William Johnson, a book of prayers of Washington, in his own handwriting, was sold at auction in 1891. The book was part of some Washington possessions that had been owned by Lawrence Washington, Thomas Washington, Bushrod Washington, and J.R.C. Lewis. It is not known whether Washington composed the prayers himself, or copied them (Johnson 23).

Among the prayers found include Washington's request that God pardon him of his sins, and "remove them from thy presence, as far as the east is from the west, and accept me for the merits of thy son Jesus Christ, that when I come into thy temple and compass thine altar, my prayers may come before thee as incense" (Johnson 25). As Commander-in-chief, he expressed the wish that every officer and man in the army would act as "becomes a Christian soldier," and refrain from the "wicked practice of profane cursing" (Gragg 56-57).

Perhaps the family of Washington felt comfortable in adding the verse from John's gospel because of this prayer, in which he spoke of Jesus Christ as one "who lay down in the Grave and arose again for us, Jesus Christ our Lord, Amen."

In the prayers, Washington repeatedly asks for "forgiveness of sins," and acknowledges the "sacrifice of Jesus Christ offered upon the cross for me." He asks that God would "frame" him more and more "into the likeness of thy son, Jesus Christ." He thanks God for giving him "assurance of salvation" (Johnson 28).

The salvation of others is also expressed in the prayers, including "the whole race of mankind." The blood of Jesus Christ is acknowledged as having the power to "wash" away his own sins, some sins of commission, but also sins of omission. His prayers look forward to the day "when the trumpet shall sound, and the dead shall arise and stand before the judgment seat, and give an account of whatever they have done in the body" (Johnson 34).

There is testimony that Washington regularly offered prayers before his meals in his home. When his step-daughter Patsy died in 1773 of "consumption," Washington beseeched the Lord to heal her, with tears in his eyes (Johnson 61).

Washington clearly believed that God had given victory to the United States, believing the perseverance of the army was a "miracle" (Gragg 209). In 1778, Washington was already making note of God's role. "The hand of Providence has been so conspicuous in all this, that he must be worse than an infidel that lacks faith, and more than wicked, that has not gratitude enough to acknowledge his obligations," Washington said on August 20, 1778. Believing that he was, at best, only "an instrument in the hands of Providence," he continued to maintain God's protection of America during his first term as president. "I am sure there never was a people who had more reason to acknowledge a divine interposition in their affairs, than those in the United States, and I should be pained to believe that they have forgotten that agency, which was so often manifested during our Revolution, or that they failed to consider the omnipotence of that God who is alone able to protect them" (Gragg 1).

In Washington's Farewell Address, published near the end of his presidency in several newspapers across the land, he offered his wisdom to the nation. "Of all the disposition and habits which lead to political prosperity, Religion and Morality are indispensable supports," arguing that it would be "vain" to claim patriotism, without "these great pillars of human happiness." Furthermore, he wrote, "And let us with caution indulge the supposition that morality can be maintained without religion," adding that "morality is a necessary spring of popular government." It is simply inconceivable that the "religion" that Washington contended would prop up popular government was some dry deism, devoid of the God who intervenes in human history.

In contrast, President Barack Obam has repeatedly quoted the Declaration of Independence, deleting "by their Creator" from the famous passage which declares "all men are endowed by their Creator with certain unalienable rights."

Historian Jared Sparks published *The Writings of George Washington* in the 1830s, and wrote to Nelly Custis-Lewis, the granddaughter of George and Martha Washington, inquiring as to the matter of Washington's religious views. Nelly was the daughter of Washington's step-son, John Custis. Nelly was adopted by George and Martha after John's untimely death, and she lived with them at Mount Vernon from the time of her birth in 1779, until her marriage in 1799, which took place shortly before Washington's death on December 14, 1799. Nelly considered them her "beloved parents."

Nelly's response to Sparks is available through several sources, and can be read in full. In the 1833 letter, she told Sparks that her grandfather had a pew in Pohick Church, where he served for many years as a vestryman of the church. He was "instrumental" in establishing Pohick Church, and contributed financially to its success. "He attended the church at Alexandria when the weather and roads permitted a ride of ten miles. In New York and Philadelphia he never omitted attendance at church in the morning, unless detained by indisposition."

Nelly recalled her aunt's illness, and Washington's fervent prayers for her recovery. While she told Sparks that she was not present at her death, she wrote that this was what she was told by several persons who *were* present.

Remarking that Washington's wife, Martha, was a very devout Christian, Nelly recalled that Martha felt assured at his death that her husband was now experiencing "happiness in Heaven."

In conclusion of her letter, Nelly Custis-Lewis asked, "Is it necessary that anyone should certify 'George Washington avowed himself to me a believer in Christianity?' As well may we question his patriotism, his heroic, disinterested devotion to his country" (http:www.christiananswers.net)

Despite powerful evidence that Washington was a Christian, there are skeptics. They argue that Washington often left church before the communion service. While this is true, it is also true that Washington *did* take communion, many times. One can speculate as to why Washington did not *always* take communion. Perhaps he took the verses in First Corinthians, in which the Apostle Paul declared that a person who ate the bread, and drank the cup, unworthily, was guilty of the body and blood of the Lord. This was a fairly common view at the time, to not participate in the service, if one considered oneself "unworthy." But, we can only speculate.

Others point to Washington's frequent public references to God as the "Author of Life," or as "Divine Providence," and other such expressions which, to the modern ear, seem to be less personal. While such language may not be in fashion today, this does *not* mean that Washington saw God as an impersonal deity, as described by the deists of his day.

As Nelly Custis-Lewis wrote to Sparks, "I should have thought it the greatest heresy to doubt his firm belief in Christianity. His life, his writings, prove that he was a Christian. He was not one of those who . . . pray that they may be seen of men. He communed with his God in secret" (Custis-Lewis).

To insist that Washington was a deist, despite such overwhelming contrary evidence is ludicrous. So why is this done? Many, of course, simply repeat what they have heard, and ignorance is their only excuse. But, why are such falsehoods perpetrated by those who should know better? Some simply want to tear down the "great man" of American history, and bring him down to their own level. After all, if George Washington rejected biblical Christianity, it reinforces their inclination to follow suit.

We should hasten to add that if one is a Christian, one's faith is not dependent upon what Washington thought, or what any of the other founders believed. But distortions of history should be corrected, including those that are perpetuated to advance some secular agenda. As Paul Gottfried wrote in the *American Conservative*, "The fact that he [Washington] and other founders include in their addresses stern affirmations on the link between religious faith and social virtue indicate that they were not smirking at Christian theology, whatever their private reservations" (Gottfried). Gottfried commented that Washington issued a Thanksgiving proclamation, extolling "our blessed religion," adding that any president who issued such a statement today would probably be attacked "for hate speech" (Gottfried).

After reading numerous letters Washington wrote to various persons over the course of his life, the historian Jared Sparks concluded, "To say that he was not a Christian would be to impeach his sincerity and honesty. Of all men in the world, Washington was certainly the last whom any one would charge with dissimulation or indirectness; and if he was so scrupulous in avoiding even a shadow of these faults in every known act of his life, however unimportant, is it likely, is it credible, that in a matter of the highest and most serious importance he should practice through a long series of years a deliberate deception upon his friends and the public? It is neither credible nor possible" (Sparks).

It is not credible. In a letter written in 1778, during the War for Independence, in which Washington had witnessed what he considered divine intervention in the survival of his rag-tag Continental Army, he wrote, "The Hand of Providence has been so conspicuous in all this, that he must be worse than an infidel that lacks faith, and more than wicked, that has not gratitude enough to acknowledge his obligations" (Fitzpatrick 343).

Anyone who could write that was no deist, at least not an honest one. Perhaps that is why it is very appropriate that the bodily resurrection of the Christian faith is affirmed at Washington's grave, and why it is that at the very top of the Washington Memorial in the city which bears his name, in Latin, are the words, "Praise to God."

Conclusion: Washington was a Christian, not a deist.

LIBEL #2

THOMAS JEFFERSON HAD CHILDEN BY HIS SLAVE

Thomas Jefferson is rightly placed on the short list of the greatest persons in American history. The fact that Jefferson served as the third president of the United States is not even on his tombstone. Jefferson, the man who doubled the size of the United States with the Louisiana Purchase during a successful presidency, instead considered his role in the establishment of the Virginia Statue of Religious Liberty, the creation of the University of Virginia, and, of course, his authorship of the Declaration of Independence as his greatest contributions to America.

The words of the Declaration of Independence still stir not only Americans but peoples striving for liberty all over the world. "We hold these truths to be self-evident, that all men are created equal," wrote Jefferson in the document we remember with all the fireworks on the fourth of July.

Yet, those very words now haunt the historical reputation of Jefferson. The man who boldly declared that all men have equal rights, a gift from God Himself, owned slaves, denying even basic human liberty to some fellow human beings. That is enough to diminish his historical reputation, but the accusation that he fathered at least one child, and probably several by one of his slaves, Sally Hemings, has severely blackened his reputation.

The charge is not new, going back to the days when Jefferson resided in the White House. Because the rumor originated from a man of questionable reputation, a known political enemy, infamous for his vicious smear tactics, it was routine for most historians to dismiss the charge. Even claims by a son of Sally Hemings that Thomas Jefferson was his father were easily refuted. After all, how would her son know about an alleged sexual relationship between his mother and the Master of Monticello, which had to have taken place before his birth?

Thomas Jefferson's wife, Patty Wayles Skelton, died young, following a difficult pregnancy. On her deathbed, she extracted a promise from Jefferson that he would never marry again. It was a promise that Jefferson honored until his own death, ironically enough, on the 50th anniversary of the adoption of the Declaration of Independence, on July 4, 1826.

Was he able to remain a widower for over 40 years because his relationship with one of his own slaves satisfied his need for female companionship?

In 1976, historian Fawn M. Brodie made the case in her *Thomas Jefferson, An Intimate History*, that Jefferson's supposed affair with Sally began while he served as our minister to France in the 1780s, when she was still in her teens. According to Brodie, Jefferson was actually talking about Sally's smooth Mulatto contours in his 25 pages of notes from his 1788 tour in France and Germany. Brodie charged that Jefferson's references, *eight times*, to the mulatto soil of the hills and valleys of those two countries, were really not about soil, but rather his mixed-blood slave concubine (294-300).

Despite this book's explosive thesis that Jefferson had taken the 14-year-old Sally to Paris with him and his daughters, and commenced the sexual relationship then, fathering a child with her in France, the ugly accusation received little traction until the release of DNA findings in 1998, in the English journal, *Nature*. The magazine article reporting the DNA "match" of a male descendant of Sally's son, Eston Hemings, and a "Jefferson male," were presented as the proof of a nearly two-hundred year old rumor of Jefferson's relationship with a slave girl.

The motivation for the DNA tests were to examine the validity of the vile rumors which first circulated while Jefferson served as president. James Callender enlisted in the new Republican Party that Jefferson had launched to combat what Jefferson saw as the monarchial tendencies of President Washington's Secretary of the Treasury, Alexander Hamilton. In 1796, Vice President John Adams, carrying the banner of the Federalist Party, narrowly defeated former Secretary of State Thomas Jefferson in the first presidential election in which George Washington was not considered.

For those who are aghast at modern politics, viewing it as a rough and tumble business, smears and accusations are not recent innovations.

In an effort to silence dissent from Jefferson's Republicans, the Federalists in Congress passed the Sedition Act, which made it a crime to write or publish false or scandalous material about certain high government officials. Interestingly, while Federalist President John Adams and his Cabinet received protection in the law from "seditious libel," along with Federalist congressional leaders, Vice President Jefferson was not afforded any such protection. (At that time, the second-highest vote-getter in the Electoral College became vice-president).

Callender was among several Republican critics that were convicted before Federalist judges for violation of the Sedition Act. Jefferson and his political ally, James Madison, secretly penned the Kentucky and Virginia Resolutions, which condemned the act, and pronounced the ability of states to "nullify," or refuse to enforce unconstitutional laws. Madison and Jefferson were frustrated that Federalist judges saw no constitutional problem with the Sedition Act. This was despite the First Amendment, ratified only *seven years earlier*, which clearly said that Congress could make *no law* abridging either freedom of speech or of the press.

When Jefferson won the presidential election of 1800 over Adams, he immediately pardoned those who had been convicted under the odious Sedition Act. (The Federalist-run Congress which had enacted the law shrewdly provided for its expiration one day into the next president's term, probably fearing that the Republicans, if they won, could then use their law to silence Federalist critics). Callender expected to receive a post mastership in the new Jefferson Administration, but Jefferson declined to make the appointment, believing Callender was unworthy. Another Callender complaint was that his demand for repayment of a fine imposed by Associate Supreme Court Justice Samuel Chase had not been honored by Jefferson's Republican Party (Bernstein 154).

Now, Callender's specialty of smearing political opposition was directed at Jefferson himself. In *The Richmond Recorder* (a Federalist newspaper) of September 1802, Callender took his revenge on what he regarded as the ungrateful Jefferson. "By this wench Sally," Callender wrote, "our president has had several children. There is not an individual in the neighborhood of Charlottesville who does not believe the story; and not a few who know it" (Meacham 217).

Callender claimed that one child was aptly named "Tom," who, Callender suggested not only bore the same name as the president of the United States, but even closely resembled Jefferson. Callender's sordid writing career came to an early end the next year when, while in a state of intoxication, he drowned. Most voters at the time who heard the story simply dismissed it as the rantings of a disgruntled failed office-seeker (Bernstein 154).

Jefferson never publicly responded to the charges, but in 1805 he did write Secretary of the Navy Robert Smith about some of the more vicious of the accusations directed at him by political opponents. He told Smith that he was guilty of only "one" of their charges, the attempted courtship of a married woman before he married his late wife. Because of the sexual nature of the admission, it can be fairly presumed that Jefferson denied any other sexually-related scandal, especially one involving a slave woman (Bernstein 156).

After Callender's death, it was Sally's son, Madison Hemings who did the most to keep the story alive. In 1873, he was interviewed by an anti-Southern Democrat abolitionist newspaper in Ohio. In the 1873 interview, in which Hemings claimed Thomas Jefferson as his father, he mostly repeated the charges of Callender, even using identical misspellings. Interestingly, Madison Hemings never actually said in the interview that his mother *told him* that Jefferson was his father. Yet, he insisted that the affair between his mother and Jefferson began shortly after the two arrived in Paris in the 1780s (Hyland 89-90).

Jefferson biographer Dumas Malone dismissed the interview as "abolitionist propaganda," adding amazement that any *real* scholar could give serious consideration to the Brodie book (Hyland 90).

Despite strong opposition from professional historians, Brodie was able to persuade *some* descendants of Sally Hemings and *some* descendants of Thomas Jefferson's *uncle* to submit to a DNA test. In a scientific DNA test, the samples must come from those in the direct male line, or male-to-male all the way from the person in the distant past to the present. *No DNA from Thomas Jefferson was possible, as he had no living "direct male" descendants* (Hyland 17).

Because DNA could not be obtained from a direct descendant of Thomas Jefferson, DNA samples were taken from a direct male descendant of

Thomas Jefferson's uncle, Field Jefferson. Another sample was obtained from direct male descendants of Eston Hemings, Sally's youngest son, and another from direct male descendants of two of Jefferson's nephews, Peter and Samuel Carr. Finally, a DNA sample was taken from a direct male descendant of Thomas Woodson. Woodson's descendants had long contended that they *were* descended from President Jefferson, but Eston Heming's descendants had never made such a claim (Hyland 19).

The conclusions were (1) Eston Hemings was the child of a male member of the Jefferson family; (2) neither Peter nor Samuel Carr could have fathered Eston Hemings; and (3) Thomas Woodson was *not* a descendant of Thomas Jefferson. The third conclusion would appear to discount that the "Tom" described by Callender in his initial 1802 article as Jefferson's child, had any scientific basis at all. If Tom, who seems to have been the right age to have been the child Sally conceived in France, was indeed the child in question, this disproved the thesis that Jefferson fathered a child with Sally while in Paris. Thomas Woodson's father was, according to DNA analysis, a Caucasian (they have many of those in France), but was most definitely *not* Thomas Jefferson (Bernstein 196).

The reason that DNA was taken from the descendants of Jefferson's nephews Peter and Samuel Carr was because they were long rumored to have fathered children by Sally Hemings. The revelation that Eston Hemings *was* descended from a "Jefferson male," or someone related to Thomas Jefferson's paternal uncle, Field Jefferson, created an immediate sensation.

Family of Eston Hemings had always heard the story that they were descended from a Thomas Jefferson "uncle." Like many family history stories passed from generation to generation to generation, they often contain some truth, mixed with some embellishment or misunderstanding. But, it is not possible that Field Jefferson, for example, could have fathered Eston Hemings because Field had died several years *before* Eston Hemings' conception. Another paternal uncle of Jefferson's had likewise died years earlier.

The commission which conducted the DNA work concluded: "After a careful review of all the evidence, the commission agrees unanimously that the allegation [note: the charge that Thomas Jefferson was the father of Eston Hemings] is by no means proven; and we find that it is regrettable that public confusion about the 1998 DNA testing and other evidence has misled many people" (Hyland 79).

Despite these words, the spin that the *Nature* article placed on the DNA findings, the way the media chose to report those findings, and the conclusions reached by other sloppy writers since, have led to the widespread perception that Thomas Jefferson essentially committed statutory rape of a teen-age girl in Paris, continued the affair for several years after his return to Virginia, and fathered several children by a slave woman, over whom he exercised legal control.

Doctor Eugene Foster, who conducted the DNA tests by using five male-line descendants of Jefferson's uncle, Field Jefferson, descendants of the Carr brothers, descendants of the slave Thomas Woodson, and one male-line descendant of Eston Hemings, the youngest child of Sally Hemings, later wrote that he was "embarrassed by the blatant spin of the *Nature* article" (Hyland 18).

Foster said, "the genetic findings . . . do not prove that Thomas Jefferson was the father of one of Sally Hemings' children . . . We have never made that claim." He added, "My experience with this matter so far tells me that no matter how often I repeat it, it will not stop the media from saying what they want to in order to try to increase their circulation . . . I am angered by it" (Hyland 19).

Yet, if the DNA indicates that a male of the Jefferson line *was* the father of Eston Hemings, then who else besides Thomas Jefferson is a logical candidate for his father?

The Jefferson Foundation noted, "Dissenters have pointed to Jefferson's younger brother, Randolph Jefferson, as a candidate for paternity, a possibility that would fit the DNA finding." It should be reiterated that the DNA findings were *not* that Thomas Jefferson was the father of Eston Hemings, but rather that a "Jefferson male" was an ancestor of Eston Hemings (Meacham 522).

Randolph Jefferson had earned a reputation for socializing with Jefferson's slaves, and was expected to visit Monticello approximately nine months before the birth of Eston Hemings (Hyland 30-33).

Until 1976, the descendants of Eston Hemings had believed that they were descended from a Jefferson "uncle." While Randolph Jefferson was Jefferson's *brother*, not his *uncle*, this is the type of thing that often occurs in family stories. Randolph was known at Monticello as "Uncle Randolph," because, of course, he *was* the uncle of Thomas Jefferson's acknowledged children by his late wife. According to Martha Jefferson Randolph, her father's younger brother was "Uncle Randolph," and he was always referred to that way in family letters (Barton 11)

Isaac Jefferson, a former slave of Jefferson's, later recalled that Randolph "used to come out among the black people, play the fiddle, and dance half the night." Thomas Jefferson, on the other hand, was 65 years old when Eston was conceived. While it is not proven that Randolph was Eston's father, it is clearly more likely than saying Thomas Jefferson was Eston's father.

The reason that Jefferson's nephews, Peter and Samuel Carr, were considered in the DNA tests, is that Ellen Jefferson, Thomas Jefferson's granddaughter, said that the Carr brothers had admitted to fathering *some* of Sally Hemings' children. The DNA tests concluded, however, that neither could have been the father of Eston Hemings (Hyland 56-57).

Despite the scant evidence against Thomas Jefferson, media reports at the time pronounced him guilty as charged. *US News Online* said, "The evidence . . . removes any shadow of doubt that Thomas Jefferson sired at least one son by Sally Hemings," while the *Washington Post* asserted the genetic testing "almost certainly proves our third president fathered at least one child by Sally Hemings." These reports were typical (Barton 6).

Why would media rush to convict Jefferson on such flimsy evidence? Part of the answer is no doubt that the media loves sensationalistic stories, which sells magazines and newspapers. After all, it is a bigger story to proclaim Jefferson fathered children by a slave woman than to say that he probably did not. Another reason is that the *Nature* article was rushed into print during the Clinton sex scandals. Henry Gee, a staff writer at *Nature*, said, "If President William Jefferson Clinton has cause to curse the invention of DNA fingerprinting, the latest report shows that it has a long reach indeed" (Barton 2).

The argument from Clinton's defenders was that if such a revered historical figure as Jefferson could have fathered children by a slave woman, shouldn't Clinton get a break for having had a sexual relationship in the Oval Office with an intern?

Clearly, the advocates of the Thomas Jefferson fathered Sally Hemings' children thesis must strain the evidence to reach the conclusion they have. For example, Jon Meacham, in his *Thomas Jefferson, The Art of Power*, said that one "suspects" that Jefferson was "in his imagination" thinking of Sally when he saw the painting of Abraham and his servant woman Hagar during his visit to Dusseldorf while in Europe. In another place, Meacham asserted, with no evidence, of course, "In this tempestuous time, Jefferson apparently began a sexual relationship" with Sally. Meacham even speculates that Sally may have reminded Jefferson of his late wife. And on it goes (Meacham 215-217).

For those who dare to deny the Jefferson-Hemings Thesis, Meacham basically dismisses them as racists, calling the liason as one "long denied by mainstream white historians" (507).

In similar fashion, Annette Gordon-Reed, in her *Thomas Jefferson and Sally Hemings: An American Controversy*, said that Jefferson scholars had long rejected the Hemings claims as nothing but "slave lies" (Meacham 195).

However, Jefferson's political opponent John Adams believed that Callender's ugly accusations were "mere clouds of unsubstantiated vapor" (Hyland 13).

Noted historian Forrest McDonald, a devotee of the greatness of Jefferson's arch-nemesis, Alexander Hamilton, was once inclined to believe the rumors, but after carefully reviewing all the evidence, including the 1998 DNA findings, concluded: "I'm always delighted to hear the worst about Thomas Jefferson. It's just that this particular thing won't wash" (Hyland 78).

LIBEL #3

JAMES POLK WENT TO WAR AGAINST MEXICO TO OBTAIN TEXAS

I settled into the chair for a long-overdue haircut, and the young Hispanic woman struck up a conversation as hair-cutters are prone to do. Predictably, she inquired as to what I did for a living, and I told her that I was a college history professor. After a few more such questions, she asked me "when it was" that the United States had "taken" Texas from Mexico.

I considered my response for a moment. "Well, actually, the United States did not *take* Texas from Mexico. Texas won its independence from Mexico in the Texas Revolution, and it was almost a decade later that Texas was admitted into the United States as a state."

She was clearly perplexed, and I offered, "Perhaps you are thinking of California, which Mexico lost in the war with the United States in 1848."

The young woman had learned her history in Mexico before her family moved to the United States. I had to wonder just what is taught in the schools of Mexico about the circumstances in which the Republic of Mexico lost Texas, with it only later becoming a state in the United States. Actually, I doubt if it is a whole lot different from what is taught in the schools *north* of the Rio Grande River. The belief that the United States went to war so as to tear Texas away from Mexico is widely held on both sides of the border, and it is yet another example of what I call historical libel, with President James Knox Polk cast as the arch-villain in the whole affair.

But it is not true.

The genesis of the Mexican War can be traced to the Louisiana Purchase of 1803, when President Thomas Jefferson bought the Louisiana Territory from France for $15 million in gold. When the American negotiators asked for more specific boundaries for Louisiana, the wily French foreign minister, Charles Maurice de Talleyrand, craftily replied, "I am sure that you Americans will make the most of it."

The boundary question resulted in some friction with Spain, whose colonial empire included both Florida and Texas. While the United States did not challenge Spain's rightful ownership of Florida, Texas was another matter. For several years, due to the uncertainty of the boundary of Louisiana, Texas remained a point of contention between the United States and Spain. The United States, however, had a more immediate concern about Spanish Florida than they did Texas. Florida was a base for Indian raids into Georgia, and was a convenient hiding place for outlaws, and runaway slaves. Of most importance, the United States feared the presence of a hostile European power on it immediate south.

President James Monroe directed John Quincy Adams, the secretary of state, to work out, if at all possible, an American purchase of Florida. Spain was willing to sell Florida, but they wanted more than just money. They wanted the Americans to cede any claim to Texas. American desire for Florida was so great that the agreement was struck, and this appeared to settle the Texas question, in 1819.

Two years later, Mexico, inspired by the success of the American secession from the British Empire, likewise won its independence from the Spanish Empire. Texas was now recognized as part of the new Mexican nation.

At the time, Texas was a very lightly populated area, with few Mexican citizens, who were vastly outnumbered by various Indian tribes, most notably the war-like Comanches. Largely for the purpose of providing a counter to the Comanches, the Mexican government made an agreement with Moses Austin, a Missouri banker, to use a tract of land in south Texas to attract immigration from the United States. These land-hungry immigrants would, however, be required to swear loyalty to the government of Mexico, and join the Roman Catholic Church.

Upon the death of Moses Austin, his son Stephen took over and accomplished most of the organizational work in 1823. In a short period of time, the American immigrants (often called Texicans or Texians) outnumbered the ethnic Mexican population by about 10-1. The political situation in Mexico appeared tolerable to the American immigrants, at first. The Mexican Emperor Augustin de Iturbide was deposed, and a constitution was adopted in 1824, deliberately modeled after that of the United

States. Iturbide was a *Centralist*, who wanted most power to be held by a central government, but the *Federalists* won out, and their constitution provided for robust protections of civil liberty and private property (Faulk 2).

The next few years saw little political discontent in Texas among either the Texians or the native Mexican community. Unfortunately, the results of the 1828 election were cast aside in a Centralist *coup d'etat* led by Anastaci Bustamante. This eventually touched off a rebellion from Federalist forces, who ousted Bustamante in 1832, then won an election in January, 1833. The Mexican Congress remained Centralist, however, which led Antonio Lopez de Santa Anna to rally Federalist forces, even gaining support from many of the powerful American immigrants in Texas, like Jim Bowie. Santa Anna's supposed devotion to federalism and constitutional government was just a ruse to gain power, however, and this led Americans in Texas to begin consideration of their own secession effort (Faulk 45-46).

Most Americans who settled in Texas were Protestant Christians, and resented the requirement of allegiance to the Roman Catholic Church. Santa Anna established a military dictatorship in 1835, further centralized power in Mexico City, abolished the Mexican Congress, rejected the Mexican Constitution, and increased the number of soldiers in Texas. Like most tyrants, he confiscated many privately-owned guns, and suppressed efforts of the Texicans to form militias. In a letter to Joel Poinsett, the U.S. minister to Mexico, Santa Anna justified these dictatorial actions, arguing that the Mexican people were not "fit for liberty," and that a "despotism is the proper form of government for them."

Austin traveled to Mexico City, hoping to avoid war. Santa Anna was in no mood to negotiate anything, and simply threw Austin in jail for several months. When Austin finally made it back to Texas, he was a changed man. Previously, he had counseled peace, but now he supported a call for independence.

Texas declared its independence in early 1836, with strong support from the ethnic Mexican community in Texas, which largely detested the dictator, Santa Anna. The new vice president of the Texas Republic, for example, was Lorenzo de Zavala. Hardly an English name!

Santa Anna was enraged, and led an army north, determined to crush the rebellion. Styling himself the "Napoleon of the West," Santa Anna did succeed in recapturing the Alamo. Texian forces under Jim Bowie had earlier taken the Catholic mission and fort away from a small Mexican garrison. It took Santa Anna's army *thirteen days* to capture the Alamo, with the loss of several hundred of his own men, but he wrote in his diary that it was "a small affair." After taking the fort, he killed all defenders who had not died in the battle, including the famed trio of William Barrett Travis, David Crockett, and Jim Bowie. It is noteworthy that seven of the defenders of the Alamo were ethnic Mexicans, who apparently shared the American immigrant's desire for liberty and self-government.

A few days later, a Texas force of about 400 surrendered at Goliad, hoping to avoid the post-battle slaughter of the Alamo. It was to no avail, and they were summarily shot. The Goliad Massacre, combined with the heroic defense of the Alamo, galvanized Texians, and led to a surge of new recruits for the Texas army, now led by General Sam Houston, a former governor of Tennessee, who had moved into Texas only a few years earlier. On April 21, 1836, Houston surprised Santa Anna and routed his army at the Battle of San Jacinto.

Houston forced the captured Santa Anna to recognize the independence of Texas, *with its border as the Rio Grande River.* President Andrew Jackson of the United States quickly recognized the independence of the Republic of Texas near the end of his term of office in early 1837. Britain and France also gave formal recognition to the Texas Republic.

What most Texans desired was admission into the United States as a state. Jackson balked at this, however, as did his immediate successor, Martin Van Buren. The United States had only a small army, and Mexico made it very clear that annexation of Texas by the United States would mean war. Additional resistance came from many northern states, where many feared Texas would be another state that would legalize slavery. Following Santa Anna's ouster as dictator, subsequent Mexican governments refused to accept the loss of Texas and rejected the recognition of Texas' independence by Santa Anna.

Mexico made feeble attempts to invade Texas over the next few years, loudly informing the United States that any attempt to annex Texas would mean the immediate breaking of diplomatic relations, followed by war.

While the annexation of Texas was shelved, largely to avoid war with Mexico, other issues led to a worsening of relations between the United States and Mexico. A chronic problem was the "claims issue," in which Mexico owed damages to American citizens, totaling about $3 million. During the Mexican independence effort against Spain, property of American citizens had been damaged. President John Quincy Adams had tried to settle the claims issue with Mexico, but was unable to get any movement from south of the Rio Grande. The next president, Andrew Jackson, likewise failed to settle the lingering dispute (Faulk 36).

Finally, the exasperated Jackson Administration broke diplomatic relations with Mexico in 1836. In 1839, relations were restored when Mexico accepted the decision of an international tribunal Mexico did owe the claims. Appealing to popular opinion inside the country, Mexican politicians dragged their feet, and made only three of the 20 payments scheduled over the next five years. Finally, they simply refused to make any more payments (Faulk 34).

Another issue that caused friction with the United States was the American desire to purchase California, so as to secure a western port. At the time, almost no Mexican citizens resided in California, which had no schools, no newspapers, no postal system, almost no police force, or courts, few books, and suffered from frequent Indian raids. According to Odie Faulk, in his book, *The Mexican War, Changing Interpretations*, there was little communication with the government of Mexico City. Alarming for the United States, the British and the French were both clearly interested in obtaining California, and the British could use their territory in northern Oregon form which to launch an invasion (Faulk 3).

Resentment toward the wealthier United States was frequently used for domestic political advantage for Mexican politicians, which only further fanned the flames of hostility.

Texan frustration at the failure of the United States to consider annexation, and fear that Mexico was going to launch yet another invasion, led the Texas government to open negotiations with France and Great Britain, for the purpose of entering into some sort of alliance with one of those two nations. This concern that Texas might become part of the British Empire contributed to a resurgence of Texas Annexation as a political issue in the United States.

Then, in 1844, Democrat presidential candidate James Knox Polk of Tennessee made the annexation of Texas a campaign issue. Almost a decade had passed, making it very difficult to reasonably argue that the United States had acted recklessly, or aggressively, risking war with Mexico over Texas. Polk's opponent, the great Whig, Henry Clay of Kentucky, ran a cautious campaign, and was much less clear as to what he would do about Texas annexation.

Polk won the election of 1844, and outgoing Whig President John Tyler submitted the Texas question to Congress shortly before Polk was to take office. On his last full day in office, Tyler signed the resolution that added Texas to the United States. Mexico fulfilled its promise to break diplomatic relations, and war seemed likely. In the 19th century, the breaking of diplomatic relations was a typical prelude to war.

But President Polk did not want war with Mexico, still hoping for a peaceful settlement of the issues dividing the neighboring nations. After several rebuffs, Polk finally received what he took as an invitation to send a diplomatic representative to Mexico City to discuss terms. But, finding a government in Mexico City with which to negotiate proved to be a problem. The presidency of Mexico changed hands *four times* in 1846 alone. Nevertheless, still hoping to avert war, Polk dispatched veteran diplomat John Slidell to Mexico City with an offer to buy Upper California and New Mexico for $25 million, the establishment of the Rio Grande as the boundary between Mexico and the U.S. state of Texas, with America promising to take over and pay the $3 million claims themselves.

Polk had reason to believe the Mexican government might be open to such an offer, as the government there was teetering on bankruptcy. But, by the time Slidell arrived in Mexico City, his very presence infuriated Mexican politicians. President Jose Herrera was denounced as a traitor for even considering talking to Slidell, and he was deposed. The new government worked the populace into a war fever, and publicly promised the Mexican flag would soon fly over the White House.

At this point, Polk faced a difficult decision. While Mexico considered the Nueces River, north of the Rio Grande, as the actual boundary of Texas, and the United States insisted the boundary had been the Rio Grande since Santa Anna's cession in 1836, the Mexican government insisted that Santa Anna had acted in duress. (Sam Houston threatened to hang him if he declined to agree to terms). Besides, the Mexican government argued, Santa Anna was no longer in power, and was not even in Mexico, having lived in exile in Cuba, where he was presently cohabitating with a 14-year old mistress.

Of even greater importance, Mexico did not consider the land *north* of the Nueces River as belonging to Texas, either, contending that *all* of Texas was still part of the Republic of Mexico.

But the United States had now made Texas a state in the United States. Because of that, the United States had a constitutional obligation to Texas, which it owed all the states: *protection from invasion.* When Texas entered the Union in 1845, it was clear that the Rio Grande River had been its southern border for nearly a decade.

Accordingly, Polk dispatched troops to the Nueces River to protect against the expected invasion the Mexican government had been promising for months. Still hopeful for a peaceful settlement, Polk had first kept the forces under the command of General Zachary Taylor on the north side of the Nueces River. However, Polk reasoned that failure to control the land *south* of the Nueces to the Rio Grande would be a *de facto* acceptance of the Mexican position that Texas' border was the Nueces, not the Rio Grande. There was also no guarantee that Mexico would even accept the loss of Texas north of the Nueces.

One must ask the question. What else was Polk to do? Texas was now part of the United States, and the U.S. government was obligated to protect the land between the Rio Grande and the Nueces from invasion, just as much as land *north* of the Rio Grande.

Failure to protect the Texas position and land with military force would have constituted a dereliction of Polk's duty as president of the United States.

This situation in which the territory of the United States was under the threat of invasion and occupation could not go on indefinitely. For those who contend that Polk should have tried diplomacy, the retort is that he *did* try diplomacy, with the Slidell mission. It is difficult to negotiate with a government which will not even talk to you. Polk did *not* send Taylor's forces south across the Rio Grande into Mexico, but only into territory that belonged to the United States. This can hardly be considered provocative.

Polk called together his Cabinet to discuss the matter, which he believed could not continue. On April 18, 1846, Mexican President Mariano y Arrillaga wrote the commander of his "Army of the North," Pedro de Ampudia: "It is indispensable that hostilities be commenced, yourself taking the initiative against the enemy." According to Faulk in *The Mexican War*, it was five days later that Paredes declared a "defensive war" had commenced against the United States. The next day, Ampudia was replaced by General Mariano Arista, who ordered his 1600 men to cross the Rio Grande and attack American forces which were on the *north* side of the river (the American side). A small American patrol of less than 70 men under Captain William Thornton was attacked, resulting in the death of 16 American dragoons.

Polk's response was immediate, sending a war message to Congress, declaring that the Mexican government had invaded "our territory, and shed the blood of our fellow-citizens on our own soil." Since that time, Polk has been ridiculed for those words from critics. But, the fact of the matter is, American blood had been shed on American soil, by an unprovoked and surprise attack from a vastly superior Mexican force. It was on the land claimed by Texas at the time the United States had voted to annex Texas the previous year.

An attack on American soldiers *on American soil* was clearly an act of war. What else could it be?

Whig Party politicians like first-term Congressman Abraham Lincoln of Illinois, were quick to demagogue the issue, demanding that Polk tell Congress *exactly* where was this "spot" on which American blood had been shed. Lincoln was in full knowledge of these above facts, but chose to neglect his duty to an American state to protect it from a foreign invasion. As a member of Congress, it was Lincoln's duty under the Constitution (which he had sworn to uphold) to defend an American state from invasion. The spot was just as much American soil as Springfield, Illinois.

The declaration of war by Congress was overwhelming, 170-14 in the House of Representatives, and 40-2 in the Senate. Yet, the Whig Party chose to play politics with the war, and their successor party, the Republicans, did the same in the post-Civil War era. The Republicans claimed the war had simply been a conspiracy of slaveholders to add more slave territory to the republic. President Grant, who had served in the Mexican War, even had the audacity to call the war "unjust" in his autobiography. This is a reflection of the post-Civil War revisionism, in which many northerners reinterpreted pre-war events to fit their theory of the war's causes.

During the war, Whig political leaders actually met with General Zachary Taylor *in Mexico,* urging him to run for president on their ticket in the 1848 election. Despite having never bothered to vote for president before in his life, Taylor did use the popularity he won from the Mexican War to capture the White House in 1848. Another Whig general, Winfield Scott, was the party's nominee in 1852. He lost, but the Whigs saw no shame in using "Mr. Polk's War," as they called it, for partisan advantage.

Why has this *myth* that the Mexican War was the fault of President James K. Polk persisted until today?

One reason is that the Whig Party chose to create this myth, at the time, mostly for political reasons. Most of the history books were written by northerners, who in interpreting the Mexican War in the light of the Civil War, chose to perpetuate the myth that the war was no more than a land grab to add another slave state. This position became accepted dogma, as illustrated by General Grant's "unjust" comments in his memoirs.

What is truly unjust is the libel perpetrated against President Polk, with the unfounded claim that Polk launched the war. This libel continues today as part of the template that the United States has been a nation built on the backs of slaves, American Indians, and "peace-loving" neighboring nations.

Polk is not guilty of this libel, and he should be exonerated.

LIBEL #4

HARDING WAS OUR WORST PRESIDENT

"**A**ll human ills are not curable by legislation" (Carson 235).

With these words, Warren Gamaliel Harding bluntly rejected the essence of the Progressive Era, which his election as president of the United States in 1920 brought to an abrupt end. Perhaps that in and of itself can explain the tendency of many professional historians to rank Harding as, if not our worst president, certainly among the worst of American presidents.

The Progressive Era was, at its core, a rejection of the vision of the Founding Fathers, who saw government as necessary in order to properly protect our natural, God-given rights, but something to be held in check, lest it become tyrannical. George Washington is said to have described government as a "dangerous servant and a fearful master."

Washington, Thomas Jefferson, Patrick Henry, and most of the founding generation had no illusions about the potential dangers of government. That is why they created a Constitution with a variety of checks on its powers. Among the many checks and balances were federalism, which divided powers between the states and a federal government, a system of separation of powers into three logical branches of government, and a system in which each branch held certain powers enabling it to "check" the power of the other two branches.

The progressives, on the other hand, saw government as a "positive" force, not to be feared so much as to be used to correct the alleged evils of society. By giving the vote to more individuals, government can be controlled at the ballot box, they believed. And, since the people have such control over government, they can use it to "improve" society. The progressives took a much more optimistic view of the ability of government to do good, believing that if a problem existed in society, the problem could simply be solved by passing a law.

Thus, Harding's admonition that not every societal ill can be cured by a law was a slap in the face to most of the professional historians who tend to favor the progressive viewpoint of greater government power to check alleged social evils. Whereas Harding warned, "Our most dangerous tendency is to expect too much of government," these progressive-leaning historians believe government should do *more* not less (Hayward 61).

One professional historian who is *not* a progressive, Paul Johnson, offered his opinion of the maltreatment of Harding by the professional historians: "The deconstruction of the real Harding and his reconstruction as a crook, philanderer, and sleazy no-good was an exemplary exercise in false historiography" (Hayward 58).

In reality, both from a constitutional and performance standard, Harding's record as president was actually quite good. Harding inherited a mess from the progressive Democrat President Woodrow Wilson. There was a reason that Harding won every state outside the then-solidly Democrat Party South, garnering over 60 percent of the popular vote. The 1920 Democrat presidential candidate, Governor James Cox of Ohio, was cursed with defending the Wilson record, and the voters chose Senator Warren Harding, also of Ohio, to reverse the nation's course of progressivism.

President Woodrow Wilson, a former college history professor, declared the 1920 presidential election a "solemn referendum" on the League of Nations. Cox agreed, saying that the "subject of the League of Nations, frankly, has possessed my very soul" (Grant). The U.S. Senate had twice refused to ratify the Treaty of Versailles, which had created the League, and Wilson hoped the American people would send the Senate a pro-League message in the election. Senator Harding, like many others at the time, was concerned that the League of Nations could evolve into a world government and infringe on American national sovereignty and the individual liberties long enjoyed by its citizens. If the election were indeed about the League, then it was clear the American people's "message" was a resounding no.

Harding inherited a growing national depression, and a national debt that had grown from $1 billion to $24 billion, in just a few short years. Inflation had eaten away at the value of the American dollar, resulting in a depreciation of at least 50 percent, since Wilson had become president in 1914. The Gross Domestic Product had contracted by one-fourth, wages had fallen by 20 percent, and 100,000 businesses had closed their doors (Hayward 63). The steel industry was working at 15 percent capacity in July 1921. John Tapping, president of Republic Iron and Steel, "pronounced 1921 the worst year in his company's 22-year history," as they had cut the payroll by over one-half in laying off over 13,000 workers (Grant).

In such difficult circumstances, it was certainly tempting for Harding to follow the activist course advocated by his Secretary of Commerce, Herbert Hoover. Harding opted to let the free market correct the down-turn, rejecting the government interventionist philosophy pushed by Hoover. "Here at home, we have too much encouragement given to the idea that a government is a something for nothing institution," Harding contended (Hayward 61).

Instead of following the advice of Hoover, a known "progressive Republican," Harding rolled up his sleeves and went to work, doing what a public official should do in times of economic depression. Rather than tamper with the free market economy (as Hoover and Franklin Roosevelt later did in dealing with the Great Depression), he allowed wages to fall to their natural level. Samuel Gompers fumed, "We will tolerate no reduction of wages," but it happened, anyway (Grant). Writing in his book, *The Forgotten Depression*, James Grant explained how the 1920-21 depression differed with the Great Depression a decade later. "What we can observe, even at this great distance of years, is that the price mechanism worked more freely in 1920-21 than it was allowed to do in 1929-1933."

"Whereas 92 percent of reporting firms had reduced wages in 1921, only 7 percent did so in 1930," Grant wrote.

Within a few short months, recovery had begun, and America was off on the "Roaring Twenties." Grant explained: "Having no foreknowledge of the Great Depression . . . people didn't even think to ask themselves why the depression was so relatively brief or the recovery so strong." Harding concentrated on modernizing the government's budget process, pushing through Congress the creation of the Bureau of the Budget (now the Office of Management and Budget).

From 1920-22, federal spending fell by one-half, from $6.3 billion to $3.2 billion. He signed legislation to cut the top tax rates almost in half

(Hayward 65). In Harding's first week in office, Secretary of the Treasury, Andrew Mellon, announced the administration's frugal intentions. "The nation cannot continue to spend at this shocking rate" (Grant). Harding had three fiscal goals: reduce taxes, refinance the war debt, and straighten out the debts the allies owed the treasury (Grant).

"It is unthinkable to expect a business revival and the resumption of the normal ways of peace while maintaining the excessive taxes of war," Harding said. "There is not a menace in the world today like that of growing public indebtedness and mounting public expenditures. There has seemingly grown up an impression that the public treasuries are inexhaustible things" (Grant).

Harding's predecessor, Woodrow Wilson, had jailed thousands of dissenters during the World War, including a man who had simply made a movie, "The Spirit of '76," an historical film version of the American Revolution. Federal prosecutors contended the motion picture was far too negative toward our war-time British allies. Harding began the process of pardoning many of these jailed individuals soon after settling in at the White House, including Eugene V. Debs, the Socialist Party candidate for president in 1920. While Harding detested the concept of socialism, he did not believe it was right to jail Debs for simply opposing the war. He even had Debs over to the White House for dinner.

Traveling to Birmingham, Alabama, Harding urged the nation to move away from racial divisions in the country, calling on the states to respect the civil rights of all its residents, including Black citizens. He argued that unless what Americans taught about our system of government was "a lie, you must stand for that equality." While Wilson had purged African-Americans from government jobs, Harding appointed over 100 Black Americans to government positions in his Administration (Hayward 66-67).

"The recorded progress of our Republic, materially and spiritually, in itself proves the wisdom of the inherited policy of noninvolvement in Old World affairs," Harding said, rejecting the interventionist attitudes of the progressive presidents, Democrat Wilson and fellow progressive Republican Theodore Roosevelt. "We seek no part in directing the destinies of the Old World. We do not mean to be entangled,"

Harding said, aligning himself with the non-interventionist viewpoint espoused by the Founding Fathers, such as George Washington and Thomas Jefferson. In fact, it was Harding who coined the very term, "the Founding Fathers" (Hayward 67-69).

But Harding was no isolationist, as he favored trade relations and armament reductions with foreign nations. He hosted the Washington Naval Conference of 1921, which reduced the size of the navies of the Great Powers. With that done, Harding was able to cut even more federal spending, and push for even more cuts in taxes. While Harding desired a strong national defense, he led the way to a more normal and modest peacetime force.

Harding's conservative philosophy was not created just for the 1920 presidential race. He had taken the conservative side in previous intra-party battles with the progressive Republicans. After two terms of progressivism under Teddy Roosevelt, the Republicans nominated and elected William Howard Taft in 1908. While Taft was not as strongly conservative as his son, Senator Robert A. Taft, would prove to be, he was certainly more conservative than Roosevelt. Taft rejected the creation of the Federal Reserve System, which precipitated the opposition of powerful American bankers, such as J.P. Morgan. Roosevelt emerged from retirement in 1912 to challenge Taft for the Republican Party nomination, with financial backing from Morgan and other supporters of a central banking system.

In this contest, Harding sided publicly with the more conservative Taft, even placing the president's name in nomination at the 1912 Republican National Convention. Taft won the nomination, and Harding won the sneers of Roosevelt's daughter, Alice Roosevelt Longworth, who later dismissed the dignified Harding as "a slob." Harding's detractors love to quote T.R.'s sharp-tongued daughter, not bothering to provide the context of her acidic comments.

Harding's rise to the White House should be considered an American success story. From a simple, middle-class background, Harding began his working career as a school teacher, a job he held for one year. He later called that job the toughest one he ever held. He then read *Blackstone's Commentaries*, considering a career in the law. But, he abandoned that idea as well. Harding sold casualty insurance for a short time, before buying the *Marion Star* newspaper at a sheriff's auction for only $300. And part of that was with borrowed money. He turned the *Star* into a successful business (Dean 9-10).

Eventually, Harding entered politics, serving in the Ohio Legislature, and was later elected a United States Senator in 1914. Six years later, he was elected president. Among the charges leveled at Harding are that his 1920 nomination for president was just "a fluke." According to this scenario, Harding's selection as presidential nominee was made by an elite group of power-brokers in a "smoke-filled room," and subsequently "forced" upon the Republican National Convention (Dean 53).

The reality is that Harding's nomination was the result of a planned strategy, worked out with his campaign manager, Harry Daugherty. After the expected 1920 nominee, Teddy Roosevelt, died unexpectedly in 1919, the Republican field was wide open. Several candidates emerged, including General Leonard Wood, Governor Frank Lowden of Illinois, Senator Hiram Johnson of California, Herbert Hoover of California, Nicholas Murray Butler of New York, and Governor Calvin Coolidge of Massachusetts (Dean 54).

For those who decry the influence of "big money" in presidential politics, Harding should be their hero. He actually turned down offers of money to run his campaign, preferring to be free of any such restraints that they would place upon him. The strategy of Harding and Daugherty was based on the belief that none of the several strong candidates so widely mentioned would be able to capture the nomination on the first ballot, and the convention would soon turn to someone else. Harding, a U.S. Senator from the key "swing state" of Ohio, would be a logical "second choice" of the supporters of the leading candidates (Dean 54).

Harding chose to enter only two of the 16 presidential preference primaries. These primaries were not taken all that seriously at the time, and Harding actually despised them. He did not like the "loathsome nature" of the new primary system, which forced Republicans to campaign openly against fellow Republicans, which he lamented contributed to party disunity (Dean 54-55).

Considered the most serious candidate by many was Leonard Wood, who campaigned in his army uniform, proudly carrying the banner of progressivism and Teddy Roosevelt. Harding's "favorite son" candidacy in Ohio was challenged by Wood. Harding ran on a platform of unashamed Americanism, saying Americans "must make sure our own house is in perfect order before we attempt the miracle of Old World stabilization. Call it selfishness or nationality if you will, I think it an inspiration to patriotic devotion—-to safeguard America first, to stabilize America first, to prosper America first, to think of America first, to exalt America first, to live for and revere America first" (Dean 55).

Harding managed to defeat Wood in Ohio, but was trounced in both Indiana and Montana. He considered pulling out of the presidential race, and concentrate on getting reelected to the Senate, but his wife Florence insisted that he stay in the fight, so he did (Dean 55-56).

The convention outcome developed just as Harding had hoped. No single candidate could gain enough support to win the nomination, so delegates began to consider alternatives. It is no surprise that Harding, a senator from Ohio (then, as now, an important "swing state"), would come to their minds. Calling the meeting of some party leaders that took place on the 13th floor suite of the Blackstone Hotel a "smoke-filled room" is like saying the sky is blue. All political gatherings of the day, regardless of party, had its share of cigar and pipe smokers.

While it seems obvious in retrospect that the Republican nominee would easily win, one must remember that the Democrats had won the last two presidential elections, and the Republicans were anxious to win in 1920. Ohio's Governor, James Cox, was expected to be the Democrat nominee, and in a close election, whichever candidate who won Ohio could be expected to carry the Electoral College's majority. Some thought the selection of another Ohio politician, such as the Republican Senator Warren Harding was perhaps necessary to edge out the Democrats.

Senator Reed Smoot of Utah left the meeting, which had no authority over the rest of the delegates at the convention. A reporter asked him who he expected to be the nominee, and Smoot told a reporter, "We decided on Harding." Of course, the group in the Blackstone had made no such decision, but when this was reported it gave the impression of momentum for Harding and it became a self-fulfilling prophecy. Although Harding eventually did win the nomination, the convention chairman, Senator Henry Cabot Lodge of Massachusetts, was actually pushing another candidate for the "smoke-filled room" to support (Dean 63-65).

After Harding won the nomination, his manager, Harry Daugherty, wanted to rush him out of the hotel, and onto a train bound for Ohio. Harding balked, insisting on speaking *personally* with over 100 reporters wishing to meet him. It is not surprising that the genuinely kind and personable Harding received good press coverage during the campaign, and throughout most of his presidency (Dean 74).

In an effort to unite the party, Harding appointed a Cabinet of both conservatives and progressives. Among those whom Harding won over included the second-richest man in the country, Andrew Mellon, who would serve as secretary of the treasury. Mellon conceived of the tax rate cuts that contributed greatly to the economic boom of the 1920s (Dean 84).

During his term of office, Harding was one of the most popular of presidents, and it was only after his sudden death in 1923 that public opinion began to shift. For several years, Harding had suffered from hypertension, and nothing really could be done about the condition under the medical knowledge of the day. This high blood pressure problem eventually killed him, almost certainly via a heart attack, in the summer of 1923. Harding was on a vacation, returning from Alaska to California, when he succumbed. As his body was transported back to Washington, D.C., by train, *nine million people* appeared along the railroad tracks as he passed by.

Daugherty recalled the scene at Cheyenne, in his 1932 book, *The Inside Story of the Harding Tragedy*. "(A)s the train came to a stop, a terrific storm burst, lightning flashed, thunder pealed, and the rain fell in torrents. I looked through the windows in amazement. Not a man, woman, or child sought shelter. They stood in their tracks while a band of school children sang, *Nearer My God to Thee*" (Daugherty 260).

Within a matter of months, his great popularity would be replaced with the widespread belief that Harding's Administration was shot through with scandal, that he was a failure as a president, and he was a man of unusually low morals.

To understand this transformation of Harding from a beloved president to the modern intensely negative perception of his term in office, one must first examine the role the Teapot Dome Scandal played in besmirching his historical reputation. In short, the scandal involved the eventual conviction of Harding's secretary of the interior, Albert B. Fall, for taking bribes from oil tycoons Harry Sinclair and Edward Doheny in exchange for the leasing of some oil reserves under his control at the Teapot Dome reserve in Wyoming and the Elk Hills reserve in California (Carson 253).

The oil reserves had been set aside for future use by the Navy during the Taft and Wilson Administrations. Oil was a critical resource needed for the fighting of the World War, and so-called experts at the time believed that such a limited amount of oil was in the ground that could be retrieved, that it would all be gone within a few years. But, with the coming of peace, oil was greatly needed to drive the engine of the expanding economy. As Daugherty explained, it was *Democrat* Senator Thomas J. Walsh of Montana who was the original sponsor of changes in law that allowed the transfer of the oil reserves to private oil companies. Ironically, it was Walsh who later prosecuted Fall before the Senate committee investigating possible bribery in the transactions.

Daugherty said that Walsh "argued in favor of leasing the naval oil reserves to private parties for development, on the ground that it was unwise for the government to undertake it." The Federal Leasing Act was passed in February, 1920, and was signed by President Wilson into law. The law was later amended to give the secretary of the navy complete control of all naval reserves. Environmentalists, led by progressive Senator Robert LaFollette opposed the measure (Daugherty 182-186).

Generally, the leasing of public land was under the control of the secretary of the interior, the post to which Harding appointed Fall. Fall was a United States Senator from New Mexico, and had intended to return to private business before he was asked by fellow senator and President-elect Harding to accept the post. According to *Tempest over Teapot Dome: The Story of Albert B. Fall,* Harding wanted Fall for the position because "there was more opportunity for graft and scandal connected with the disposition of public lands" than was the case in other departments, and Harding wanted "a man who is thoroughly honest" (Stratton 197).

Fall finally relented, and took the appointment. He wrote his wife, "I am now trying to look upon the bright side and see the compensations which may offer themselves in that position." While it is doubtful that Fall meant the acceptance of bribes as among those "compensations," he eventually did lease the reserves to two oil men and received "loans" of about $100,000. Fall maintained later that the loans had nothing to do with his decision to lease the reserves to Doheny and Sinclair, but a jury eventually decided otherwise, sending Fall to prison. Oddly, while Fall was convicted for *taking* bribes, Doheny and Sinclair were acquitted of *offering* bribes (Stratton 197; Carson 254).

Harding had no reason to know that Fall had taken what a jury would later decide were bribes. As Daugherty explained, "The President received from Fall a report on the leases made under him. This report contained nothing of an illegal or suspicious nature. And the secretary of the interior, concealing from the President the fact that he had secured no competitive bids and had received a 'loan' of $100,000 from Doheny before these leases were made, allowed his chief to send to the Committee a letter of endorsement (Daugherty 182-186).

If Harding should be held responsible for Fall's corruption, then perhaps the entire U.S. Senate that confirmed Fall, in less than one minute, with no hearings, without a dissenting vote, should also be held to account.

Another scandal that damaged Harding's historical reputation was found in the Veteran's Bureau. As a result of America's participation in the First World War, the United States had to deal with thousands of veterans, and the Congress created the Veteran's Bureau to handle the situation. Harding appointed Charles Forbes, a highly decorated veteran of the war, to lead the new agency. Eventually, Attorney General Daugherty suspected Forbes was selling surplus supplies at absurdly low prices to private contractors and taking kickbacks (Dean 140).

Daugherty alerted Harding about his concerns. Harding demanded that Forbes explain himself, and Forbes basically lied to the president, giving him phony information. Harding ordered Forbes to stop his sales, but Forbes did not stop. So, in February, 1923, Harding called Forbes in again and demanded his resignation for insubordination. The extent of Forbes' extensive criminal activity was not discovered until after Harding's death later that summer. If Harding is responsible for Forbes's corrupt activity, he should at least be given some credit for appointing his replacement, who cleaned up the mess.

Writing in his book, *The Growth of America, 1878-1928*, historian Clarence Carson summarized the impact of the scandals. "After all this furor, the worst that could be said about President Harding was that he used bad judgment in one or two (among numerous) appointments and in selecting one or more of his friends. That his reputation should be so badly tarnished by these wayward events does not speak well for historians who have generally downgraded his achievements" (254).

While there is no evidence that Harding knew of Fall's corruption, Harding's sudden death from an apparent heart attack, led to the unfounded speculation that he was perhaps poisoned by his own wife! This bizarre theory was championed by Gaston Means, in his scandalous book, *The Strange Death of President Harding*.

What could have led the public to believe that Florence Harding would murder her own husband?

One answer was soon provided by Nan Britton of Harding's hometown of Marion, Ohio, a woman about 30 years younger than Harding, who claimed she had carried on a long-term sexual affair with the late president. She asserted that he was the father of her child, Elizabeth Ann Christian, in her book, *The President's Daughter*, published a few years after Harding's death.

Britton certainly had a "thing" for Harding. In her high school English book, she wrote several references to Harding, who was then the local newspaper publisher in Marion. She even wrote on page one of the book that among the reasons George Washington should be honored was because "he looks like Harding" (Ferrell 50-51).

While Britton had earlier named a soldier in Europe, Edmund M. Christian, on the birth certificate as her daughter's father, in the book she said that the girl was conceived in Harding's Senate office in 1919, and that they continued the affair even after he was president, even having sex in a White House closet! (Ferrell 52-53).

The charge lacks evidence. Frank Gibbs, who traveled with Harding during the presidential campaign in 1920, said he was with Harding "almost constantly," and yet he had "never heard of a woman by the name of Nan Britton." Patrick Kenrey, the doorkeeper at the executive offices for 35 years said that not only had he "never" heard of Nan Britton, but furthermore he knew that "no strange woman ever came here to see President Warren G. Harding." Ike Hoover, who began working at the White House during the administration of President Benjamin Harrison in the 1880s, and left at the start of the administration of Franklin Roosevelt in the 1930s, was blunt: "Nan Britton is a liar" (Ferrell 58-59).

Daugherty was vehement in his denunciation of Nan Britton. "Without hesitation, therefore, I say that I never heard of her, nor heard her name spoken, until the appearance of the book, *The President's Daughter*" (Daugherty 249).

Daugherty challenged Britton's account on multiple points. He noted that Richard Wightman, who helped Britton write the book, was sued for divorce over his association with Britton. He called attention to the fact, that despite supposedly seeing Britton several times in the period before Harding was president, he never bothered to see his supposed child. "He loved children," Daugherty said. "He was never known to pass a child without a smile or a touch of his big, gentle hand" (Daugherty 249, 251).

What Daugherty found especially incredible was, that in a book of 439 pages, "there is produced not a single letter of Harding's to Miss Britton. The writer says that he was an habitual writer of love letters and sent her hundreds—-many of them forty to sixty pages long! The author of *The President's Daughter* could not produce one of these, for a simple reason. They were never written. They were never received by Miss Britton. One genuine love letter would have been enough to establish her case. But she never has and never can produce it" (Daugherty 251).

Of course, Britton claimed that she destroyed all of these supposed love letters, but Daugherty explained why the alleged affair never "came out." The reason it did not come out, was because, Daugherty insisted, "such a thing never happened" (248).

Despite his "love of children," Harding and his wife never had any children. The reason that they never had children, was that Harding was sterile. Doctor Joseph De Barthe, writing in *The Answer* in 1928, concluded

Harding was physically unable to have a child, and for that reason alone, Nan Britton's book was a lie. De Barthe asked in his book, "Would a normal flesh and blood mother cast the pestilence of a bawdy house upon her innocent offspring to gain her own financial independence?" Britton sued, but the jury took only one hour to return a verdict of "no cause for action" (Ferrell 69-70; 76).

When Gaston Means' scandalous book appeared, Daugherty predicted "the good sense of the American people" would reject it. "The attack upon Mrs. Harding and President Harding, both of whom are dead, is a disgrace to America."

"The book will appeal to those envious souls who love to see men in high places befouled when they cannot be broken, and will put soiled money in the pockets of the author" (Daugherty 227-228).

Some of the accusations made against Harding in the wake of his death were so absurd that it is amazing that any fair-minded person would repeat them today. Charges were even made that night after night, Harding and his cronies engaged in high-stakes poker games, excessive drinking, and sexual orgies, *inside the White House!*

One must wonder why this image of an incompetent and corrupt Warren Harding was created so soon after his death, and why such a false picture of the man is still repeated today, from the halls of academia to the popular culture?

It is not a surprise that liberal or progressive Democrats today would have such a low opinion of a conservative Republican president like Harding. But, probably a majority of *conservatives* who are aware of the Harding Administration of a vague, but negative opinion of the man, thinking something like, "Wasn't he involved in a lot of scandals?"

Speaking to a Republican who calls himself an admirer of the progressive Republican President Theodore Roosevelt, I referred to Harding as perhaps the most under-rated president in U.S. history. His response was a tirade of invective, concluding with the vile charge that Harding had visited every whorehouse in Washington, D.C. When I challenged his slanderous remarks by asking, "Just how do you know that?" his response was instructive: "How do you know that he did not?"

The fact of the matter is that a fair assessment of the Harding presidency and of the man himself would not lead one to the conclusion that he was a poor president, or a particularly immoral person. The evidence simply does not lead one to that conclusion.

The probable genesis of the libel that Warren Harding was both a horrible person and a horrible president is that his death occurred just on the eve of the 1924 presidential campaign. Faced with a roaring economy, and Harding's general success while in office, the Democrats desperately needed an issue, and the Teapot Dome Scandal provided that. Once the attacks began, they fed on themselves. Despite the onslaught of attacks upon a defenseless dead man, the Democrats got very little electoral help from their vicious attacks upon Harding. Harding's vice president, Calvin Coolidge, won a huge victory in the election the next year, almost completely untarnished by all the mud thrown on the memory of Warren Harding.

The Republican Party, determined to win the 1924 election, is at least partly to blame for the destruction of Harding's reputation. In an effort to deflect attention away from their president, Coolidge, and the rest of the Republican Party, Harding became the convenient scapegoat on whom to place the blame for any and all scandals. The argument used by the G.O.P. was that Coolidge was "the Puritan in Babylon." While Harding was corrupt, the Republicans conceded, "We now have a president who is totally free from corruption."

Hoping to avoid being dirtied by the ton of mud piled on top of the grave of the late Warren Harding, Republicans more or less joined in burying the reputation of a man who had returned them to the White House in 1920, and laid the foundation for landslide victories in 1924 and 1928.

Harding deserved better from his own party, and he should be exonerated from the smear that he was our worst president. On the contrary, we would be lucky to have such a man like Harding in the White House today.

LIBEL # 5

THE SCOPES TRIAL MADE A MONKEY OUT OF WILLIAM JENNINGS BRYAN

I n the popular mind, the Scopes "Monkey" Trial settled the truth of the theory of evolution, and demonstrated that the Bible is a book of fables, in contradiction to the known laws of science. Furthermore, William Jennings Bryan, a former Democratic Party candidate for president and a former secretary of state was exposed as a buffoon, a typical ignorant believer in the biblical account of creation.

This is the narrative we find in history and science textbooks, and in the popular culture. It is a narrative that was reinforced in the minds of the average person by the 1960 movie starring Frederic March as the "woefully ignorant" Bryan (called Brady in the movie), and Spencer Tracy as the "heroic, but kindly" agnostic, Clarence Darrow (called Henry Drummond in the movie).

The central problem with this portrayal is that it is not only full of falsehoods, the falsehoods are so extreme that one must wonder if the authors of the play (from which the movie was adapted) were simply mendacious. From what one saw in the movie, one would think that John T. Scopes (called Bert Cates in the film) was facing prison time for simply teaching high schools students about the Darwinian theory of evolution.

On the contrary, the Tennessee state law which forbade the teaching of the theory of evolution in the public schools as an established fact did not provide any jail time at all, but only a relatively small fine. When Charles Darwin advanced his theory that all life on earth evolved from simpler forms into modern humans, sharing common ancestry with modern apes, the average Christian gave it little thought. After all, it was a theory, and as far as they were concerned, Darwin and his disciples could think whatever they wished as to the origin of life. But, when the theory began to be taught in the public schools across America as a proven *fact* of science, conflict with Bible believers was inevitable. It was the position of many devout Christians that their hard-earned tax dollars should not be spent teaching their own children that the *biblical* account of creation was a mere fable.

The Tennessee Legislature responded to their constituents and passed a law which did not absolutely forbid the teaching of the theory of evolution, but the teaching of it as *fact*. The recently formed American Civil Liberties Union (ACLU) decided to challenge the law, asserting it was in violation of the Tennessee state Constitution by advancing a "religious" viewpoint. George Rappleyea, an engineer who managed local mines in Dayton, Tennessee, a believer in Darwinian evolution, and a Yankee transplant from New York, read of the ACLU's desire to mount a challenge to the law. He believed a legal challenge in Dayton could give a boost to the local economy (Kazin 287).

Rappleyea and the ACLU prevailed upon a Dayton High School teacher, John T. Scopes, to agree to admit to teaching Darwinian evolution, in order to test the law's constitutionality. Scopes was another Yankee, from Salem, Illinois, and he was a believer in the evolutionary viewpoint. However, it is very unlikely that Scopes ever mentioned Darwin's theory in a classroom in Dayton. First of all, Scopes was *not* the school's biology teacher, but was mainly a math teacher, who also taught physics. He was hired mainly to coach the high school football team, but he had substituted in the biology class. Michael Kazin said in his *A Godly Life* (a biography of William Jennings Bryan), that Scopes "violated unintentionally" the anti-evolution law one day while substituting for the "regular" biology teacher. In Scopes' autobiography, *Center of the Storm*, "To tell the truth, I wasn't sure I had taught evolution." He added, "If the boys had got their review of evolution from me, I was unaware of it. I didn't remember teaching it" (Kazin 285; quoted in Perloff, 28).

Yet, when the movie *Inherit the Wind* opens, Scopes (or Cates as he is called in the motion picture) is teaching not from the textbook that was actually used in Dayton, but right out of Darwin's *Descent of Man*.

This is just one of a multitude of fabrications seen in the movie that varies with the facts. One has to wonder if the authors of *Inherit the Wind* changed Scopes to Cates, Dayton to Hillsboro, Bryan to Brady, Darrow to Drummond, and so on, so as to be able to create an anti-Christian story with the ready defense that, hey, it is just fiction, if called on for one of their many blatant falsehoods. The problem with this type of gross distortion is that the movie is the extent of the average person's historical "knowledge" about the famous "Monkey Trial."

While the textbook used in the Dayton biology class, *Civic Biology*, did present the theory of evolution as a fact, evidences for the theory are rather scant in the lengthy textbook. Most of the textbook covers various living things, diseases, hygiene, and various other fairly noncontroversial topics. What *is* found in the textbook, is, however, very interesting.

For example, the student is told, "In the insect communities the welfare of the individual is given up for the best interests of the community . . . This should teach us, as we come to take our place in society, to be willing to give up our individual pleasure or selfish gain for the good of the community in which we live." So, students should learn to be more like insects? (Hunter, Kindle edition).

Evolutionists of the day, such as the textbook's author, George Hunter, contended that human beings were continuing to evolve, and that some humans were simply further advanced than others. Dayton's high schoolers could read in their textbook, that, "at the present time there exist upon the earth five races or varieties of man." Hunter explained that "the highest type of all, was the Caucasian, represented by the civilized white inhabitants of Europe and America" (Hunter).

In an effort to continue the upward evolutionary advancement that Hunter believed humans had reached with the white race, he said that certain individuals are "handicaps." Hunter contended that it was "criminal" to hand down to posterity these handicaps, such as "feeble-mindedness." He lamented that studies "have been made on a number of different families in this country, in which mental and moral defects were present in one or both of the original parents." The breeding of these persons had cost the taxpayers heavily in prisons and asylums (Hunter).

Hunter noted a specific case of a young soldier from the War of the Revolution who seduced a feeble-minded girl. The girl then produced a "feeble-minded son." By his day, Hunter noted the large number of "feeble-minded" descendants. In contrast, "The man who started this terrible line of immorality and feeble-mindedness later married a normal Quaker girl. From this couple a line of 496 descendants have come with *no* cases of feeble-mindedness." Hunter finished by explaining the lesson the students should take from this information: "The evidence and the moral speak for themselves."

Hunter called these feeble-minded persons "parasites" on society. "They not only do harm to others, but by corrupting, stealing, or spreading disease, but they are actually protected and cared for by the state out of the public money. Largely for them the poorhouse and the asylum exist. They take *from* society, but they give nothing in return. They are the true parasites."

After thus starkly stating the "problem," in his view at least, Hunter offers what he calls the "remedy."

"If such people were lower animals, we would probably kill them off to prevent them from spreading," Hunter continued, admitting that society would probably not allow such to human beings. What he suggested was that the sexes be separated in various ways, "preventing intermarriage and the possibilities of perpetuating such a low and degenerate race. Remedies of this sort have been tried successfully in Europe and are now meeting with success in this country."

Bryan had read Hunter's textbook, and he was horrified. This was a major factor in his dedication to fight the Darwinian theory. He was concerned that the general acceptance of the view that humans were simply animals, and that we could advance even higher up the evolutionary tree by discarding the parasites, would lead to horrific social consequences. So, when the trial was announced, Bryan offered to join the prosecution team, hoping to expose not only the falsity of the theory of evolution, but also the negative consequences should it become widely accepted. (Bryan's concern was well-placed as can be seen from its influence on Hitler and the National Socialists of the next decade in Germany).

The defense, financed by the ACLU on "free speech" grounds, consisted of four lawyers, but only Clarence Darrow was willing to directly attack the Bible. Other members of the defense team, such as Dudley Malone, simply argued that Scopes should be free to teach the theory of evolution, expressing no inclination to attack the veracity or authority of Scriptures. Malone pointed out that Muslim invaders had burned the great library of Alexandria on the grounds that it was not needed, since in their minds the Koran already contained all needed truth. According to Malone, students should learn all views, leaving them free to make their own decisions.

"The truth is no coward," Malone told the court (Kazan 290).

Apparently, the truth *is* a coward, when the cause is to promote Darwinian evolution. The jurors were presented with a fairly simple case. Did John Scopes teach the theory of evolution as fact, in violation of the statutes of Tennessee? Scopes apparently *lied*, and claimed that he did, in fact, teach the theory of evolution in the classroom, when he did not. As Bryan said, in opposing the introduction by the defense team of supposed scientific "evidence" for evolution, "This is not the place to try to prove that the law ought never to have been passed. The place to prove that, or teach that, was to the Legislature."

Darrow and his fellow defense lawyers decided to spring a surprise on Bryan and call on him to take the stand as an "expert" on the Bible. The judge told Bryan he could refuse, and he no doubt should have declined the challenge. Bryan told the judge he would be glad to be interrogated by Darrow, probably the most skilled criminal defense lawyer of his day, who had practiced for the moment the night before with the rest of his defense team.

Why did Bryan do this? Perhaps it was ego, perhaps it was his irritation at the attacks upon his beloved Bible he wished to refute. Bryan was one of the most effective public speakers in American history, but when he took the stand, Darrow would control the line of questioning. There was no way that Darrow was going to allow Bryan to break into the "silver-tongued oratory" that had catapulted him into national prominence at the young age of 36. Now, at 65, suffering from diabetes in the sweltering July heat of east Tennessee, Bryan was not physically prepared for the contest.

Still, the movie depicts a Bryan who was a babbling buffoon. Bryan was nothing of the sort, but those who only know about Bryan from the movie can certainly be excused for thinking so. The Bryan (or Brady as he is called in the picture) shown on the stand in the movie was not only an historically inaccurate caricature, it was libelous.

Bryan agreed to the inquisition by Darrow, on the promise that Bryan would be allowed to put Darrow and the rest of the defense team on the stand, too (Kazan 292).

Instead of asking Bryan questions about the theory of evolution, Darrow launched into an attack centered on just how literally to take the Bible. Of course, this was irrelevant to the law upon which the case was being tried.

Under questioning, Bryan refused to speculate as to how God had made the earth stand still for Joshua. In response to another question, Bryan said he did not believe the six days of Genesis were literal 24-hour days. In the movie distortion, however, Bryan is shown as responding with incredible specificity, even to the time of day that God created the earth! The movie has Darrow asking Bryan, "You're up here as an expert on the Bible. What is the biblical evaluation of sex?" with Bryan responding, "It is considered Original Sin." This was a total fabrication, as Darrow never asked about sex (Kazan 292).

Other questions that Darrow *did* ask had no bearing on the case at hand, such as how did the snake walk before it was cursed?, where did Cain get his wife?, how many people were in Egypt 3500-5000 years ago?, and so on. Of course, the Bible does not answer these questions, so it was absurd to expect Bryan to answer them, either (Cornelius 14-15).

Skeptics of the Bible often like to play with the word "literal" when challenging the Bible, and Darrow was no exception. "Do you claim that everything in the Bible should be literally interpreted?" Darrow asked. Bryan answered, "I believe everything in the bible should accepted as it is given there; some of the Bible is given illustratively. For instance: 'Ye are the salt of the earth.' I would not insist that man was actually salt, or that had flesh of salt, but is used in the sense of salt saving God's people."

The movie version does not use the actual words of Darrow or Bryan, although they are easily available. In the movie, the Darrow character asked the Bryan character, "You believe that every word written in this book should be taken literally?" and the Bryan character responds, "Everything in the Bible should be accepted, exactly as it is given there." Such distortions cannot be accidental.

Bryan was eager to get Darrow on the stand the next day, and question him over some of the problems with the Darwinian theory. Darrow wasn't about to allow that, however. Scopes' plea was changed from not guilty to guilty, ending any more testimony (Kazan 294). One can guess that Darrow had planned this all along, when he promised Bryan would have the opportunity to question him on the theory of evolution. As Scopes said in *Center of the Storm*, "Darrow had been afraid for me to get on the stand. Darrow realized that I was not a science teacher and he was afraid that if I were put on the stand I would be asked if I actually taught biology" (Perloff 28).

In the movie version, Bryan demanded to make a few "brief remarks" at the end of the trial, but the crowd leaves him while he is robotically reciting the books of the Bible. Of course, this whole scene was simply made up by the movie authors, including Bryan's physical collapse. Bryan *did* die, probably from complications of diabetes the Sunday afternoon after the trial, but not in as dramatic a fashion as in the movie, right at the conclusion of the trial.

In *Inherit the Wind*, the devout Christians are portrayed as filled with hate. This included a local minister, a created fictional character. Darrow is uniformly shown sympathetically. In real life, when told of Bryan's death, Darrow dismissed someone's lament that Bryan had died of a "broken heart," Darrow callously responded, "Broken heart, nothing. He died of a busted belly" (Koenig 658). The movie uses a version of this incident, but in the movie it is the infidel journalist H.L. Mencken (Hornbeck in the movie) who disrespectfully dismisses Bryan's death as from a "busted belly." Incredibly, the movie Darrow castigates Mencken for his hateful mocking of Bryan's demise, another fictitious scene.

Both Darrow and Mencken used name-calling and ridicule against the Christians of Dayton, rather than intellectual arguments. Before the trial began, Darrow was heard to dismiss Bryan as "the idol of all Morondom." Mencken was instrumental in creating the pro-evolutionist myth about the Scopes trial and Bryan, while the trial was progressing, in his slanted commentaries about Dayton, and its supposed ignorant Christian populace.

Bryan was certainly no ignorant buffoon. Regardless of what one thinks of his political philosophy, Bryan had been a major political figure since 1896, winning the Democrat nomination for president three times, and had served in Congress, and as secretary of state.

Bryan *was* a devout Christian, however, and that is probably enough to mark him as an intellectual pygmy by atheists and agnostics. He foresaw the negative effects upon society of a theory that taught human beings were nothing but animals, even of a higher sort. In particular, Bryan expected the viewpoint of *theistic evolution*—-the belief that God used evolution to "create" humans—-would eventually lead to *atheistic evolution*, calling theistic evolution an "anesthetic," that would make the Christian not notice any pain "while his religion is removed."

Bryan published an article in *Reader's Digest* magazine in August, 1925, written shortly before his death. In the article, Bryan took special aim at the supposed "missing link" between humans and apes, the so-called Nebraska Man.

"Someone searching for fossils in a sand hill in Nebraska came upon a lonely tooth. The body of the animal had disappeared; not even a jaw bone survived. Professor Osborn summoned a few congenial spirits, nearly as credulous as himself, and they held a post mortem examination on this insignificant tooth. After due deliberation, they announced that the tooth was the long looked-for missing link which the world awaited" (Bryan, qtd in Cornelius 27).

Not long after Bryan's death, another such tooth was found, only the animal did not look anything like an ape or a human, or anything in-between. The tooth belonged to an extinct pig.

This was yet another example of a lie, associated with the famous Monkey Trial. Perhaps the libel that Darwinian evolutionists triumphed over the "ignorant" William Jennings Bryan in 1925 is yet another libel of history that we can bury with that poor pig.

LIBEL #6

JOE McCARTHY SMEARED INNOCENT PEOPLE

I turned on my little black and white television set in my college dorm room on February 6, 1977 to watch a Sunday night movie, "Tail-Gunner Joe," about the late Senator Joseph McCarthy. My mostly apolitical roommate decided to watch the NBC broadcast with me. I was the history major, and he was a music major, so it is not surprising that I was much more aware of who McCarthy was, and what he had done, but I decided not to tell him my views on McCarthy, to see what his reaction would be, to what I expected to be liberal propaganda.

Perhaps no person in American history has been as unfairly smeared as McCarthy, a Republican senator from Wisconsin, until his death in May, 1957. The story line usually given about McCarthy in the history books and in the popular culture is that McCarthy terrorized the nation from 1950 to 1954, with Americans quaking in fear that they would be the next person falsely accused of being a Communist, and sent to prison. In fact, according to the typical but false narrative, untold numbers of good, patriotic Americans had their reputations smeared by McCarthy, and when it was all said and done, McCarthy never uncovered a single Communist anyway. Or so they claim.

I already knew quite a bit about McCarthy, although not nearly as much as I do now, after reading many books and magazine articles. But, as McCarthy's top aide, Roy Cohn, said in his book responding to the TV movie, "Tail-Gunner Joe," the movie "was not the truth, in words or in substance. And it was not intended to be the truth." It was intended as a smear, pure and simple. For all the supposed quaking in fear that McCarthy created, what Cohn said about the TV movie could be said about most academic and pop culture coverage of McCarthy: "They conceded to him not one decent human quality" (Cohn vii-viii). In his 1959 book, *Senator Joe McCarthy*, Richard Rovere even felt it important to inform us, "McCarthy belched in public" (48).

Cohn said that the movie opened and closed with a lie. Not content to challenge his accusations concerning Communist infiltration into the U.S. government, the movie even denigrated his record in World War II. McCarthy, as a judge at the time, could have claimed an exemption from service, but did not, even winning commendation from Admiral Chester Nimitz. Nimitz said that McCarthy participated in a large number of combat missions, obtained vital photographs of enemy gun positions despite intense anti-aircraft fire, and suffered a severe a severe leg injury, for which he refused to be hospitalized, continuing to carry out his duties. But NBC chose not to relate any of that, instead giving the viewers the impression that "all he did was shoot at coconuts," as Cohn said (xii-xiii).

The movie was unrelenting in its presentation of McCarthy as a uniformly despicable character. About an hour into the three-hour movie, my roommate started laughing. "What is it?" I asked. He said, "Nobody could have been this bad." At least in the case of my roommate, NBC's portrayal of McCarthy as a person totally devoid of any positive qualities had gone too far. By the time of the totally fabricated scene of a hospitalized and psychotic McCarthy using a mop defend himself from the doctors and nurses, which he took to be Communists, the movie was nothing but a comedy to my roommate.

But, in a way, it is no laughing matter. It is like the actual Joseph McCarthy never existed, and in his place is a fictional arch-villain. The myth that McCarthy terrorized the country for almost five years, smearing the reputations of uniformly innocent people, falsely accusing scores of being in league with a global Communist conspiracy, is firmly settled in the minds of most Americans. It even has a term: *McCarthyism. McCarthyism* is defined as smearing the innocent. It is noteworthy that this term was first used in the pages of the *Daily Worker*, an official newspaper of the American Communist Party.

While it would be odd that a Communist newspaper would care that McCarthy was destroying the reputations of folks who were *not* Communists, it is not surprising that the *Daily Worker* would hate a United States Senator who exhibited amazing energy and zeal in fighting Communist infiltration of the U.S. government. What is puzzling, and even disgraceful, is the darts and arrows cast at McCarthy by non-Communists, and even *conservatives*, who should know better.

Writing in *Human Events*, M. Stanton Evans, author of the definitive book on McCarthy, *Blacklisted by History*, responded to the use of the Communist-coined term of *McCarthyism* by *conservatives*. "How ironic, then, to have conservative spokesmen at talk radio shows, the blogosphere or FOX News robotically utter liberal falsehoods about McCarthy." Evans speculated that these conservative commentators gave no hint that they "know anything about the subject." Evans lamented that it "was painfully clear that the talkers knew nothing of McCarthy, but were simply reciting in half-remembered phrases the standard liberal line about him" (Evans, *Human Events* 22).

I recently read in the state newspaper of a large, conservative Christian denomination an article about former NFL football coach Tony Dungy, who is also a well-known Christian. Dungy had been attacked for offering a view that did not coincide with the accepted liberal position, and the article was entitled, "Christian McCarthyism: Tony Dungy." The article began, "There is a new McCarthyism sweeping across our cultural landscape," asserting that those who hold to a biblical worldview are the victims of this "Christian McCarthyism." The article concluded, "The new Christian McCarthyism hears only what it wants to hear."

From reading the article, it is not clear what the writer thought Joe McCarthy actually said and did way back in the 1950s, but one would hope that the author, a Christian minister, would not want to spread false information about McCarthy, in order to defend Dungy. Bearing false witness is wrong, even if it is about a person who has been dead since 1957.

So, what was McCarthy trying to accomplish? From this and similar articles, one might conclude—-incorrectly—-that McCarthy was on a crusade to smear innocent folks as members of a monstrous Communist conspiracy, and maybe even put them in a federal prison. Actually, McCarthy's goals were always narrow. His efforts were concentrated on getting Communists out of a sensitive positions in the United States government. Unless one believes a person has a right to a government job, while spying for a hostile foreign power, this seems rather commendable. Furthermore, he was troubled that the Truman Administration had not taken action to rid the government of Communist spies. And, yes, there were multitudes of Communist spies in sensitive positions inside the U.S. government, such as Alger Hiss, and the atomic spies Ethel and Julius Rosenberg.

Conservative journalist John T. Flynn noted that it was clear what McCarthy wanted to do. "McCarthy was not persecuting radicals or even Communists. His aim was at only Communists and spies *inside the American government*, including the Army" (14-15).

It is not possible to address every error ever printed about McCarthy. They multiply as though with a life of their own, as writers parrot the same errors over and over, without bothering to check the historical record for themselves. Even Evans, who wrote the most complete work on McCarthy (*Blacklisted by History*), admitted, "I haven't attempted to track down and answer every McCarthy-related error that's out there" (Evans, *Blacklisted*, 12).

To give the reader a general idea of the number of inaccuracies that abound on McCarthy, then, I will only examine three specific charges: (1) McCarthy changed his numbers of alleged Communists in the State Department; (2) McCarthy smeared the life of a poor African-American woman, Annie Lee Moss; and (3) McCarthy used a Hollywood Blacklist to ruin the careers of many talented "artists" in the motion picture industry.

The last one is the easiest to refute, because it is so clearly absurd. The way it is usually cast is that McCarthy, from his position as Chairman of the House Committee on Un-American Activities, created the Hollywood Blacklist in which certain actors, directors, producers, writers, and so on, lost their jobs in the movies, or could not find work, due to a "blacklist" that named them as Communists. And it was all the work of McCarthy.

First of all, since McCarthy was a United States Senator, it should be obvious to a moderately educated person that he was not going to be a member of a committee of the House of Representatives, much less its chairman. Furthermore, McCarthy hardly spoke of Communist subversion as an issue before 1950, and the Hollywood Blacklist was already well on its way. Finally, McCarthy did not speak out on Communists in Hollywood or in any other *private* industry, but rather expressed alarm at only those who held sensitive positions inside the United States government.

In his initial Senate campaign in 1946, McCarthy had expressed a desire to rid the government payroll of Communists, but as Arthur Herman explained in his book, *Joseph McCarthy,* the senator made little of the issue until 1950 (Herman 96-102). By then, the numbers of persons under the heel of Communist dictatorship had grown from less than 200 million to 800 million. The Rosenbergs had contributed to the Soviet A-bomb. Alger Hiss, who had been in the U.S. State Department, had been an aide to President Franklin Roosevelt, was a respected pillar of the American Establishment, but then he was uncovered as a traitorous spy for Stalin and was eventually convicted for lying under oath about his spying activities for the Soviet Union.

In February, 1950, Senator McCarthy flew to Wheeling, West Virginia, to deliver a speech as the guest of the Ohio County Republican Women's Club, on the occasion of their Lincoln Day Dinner. A little less than 300 Republican activists became witnesses to the opening of what is now called "the McCarthy Era," as McCarthy would deliver a salvo against the Truman Administration for its failure to rid the U.S. government of Soviet spies.

According to McCarthy's long-time assistant, Roy Cohn, McCarthy's interest in the issue of Communist subversion inside the government began just before Thanksgiving, in 1949. Three men, including an Army intelligence officer, were highly concerned about a 100-page document prepared by the Federal Bureau of Investigation (FBI), which listed names of individuals "known to be active in the Party," that were burrowed deep inside the agencies of the government. The men had failed to interest three other senators to take the lead on this issue, before bringing their concerns to McCarthy.

McCarthy told Cohn, after reading the document, "I have made up my mind—-I was going to take it on" (Cohn 8-10).

And take it on he did, to the startled ladies in Wheeling, West Virginia, announcing that he had "in his hand" a list of people in the State Department who were "either card-carrying Communists or certainly loyal to the Communist Party." The number of these "card-carrying" Communists, according to McCarthy, was 57. Oddly, very soon after the speech, the exact number of Communists inside the State Department that

McCarthy had claimed became a point of contention. McCarthy's detractors claimed that he had said 205, not 57, and when McCarthy later testified, under oath, before a Senate committee about the number 57, he was actually threatened with perjury!

The larger number, 205, was, in McCarthy's words, not a list, but rather a statistic. According to Evans, it came from a letter that Secretary of State James Byrnes had written in 1946 to a U.S. congressman. It appears that Byrnes had said that there were 284 State Department employees on whom security screeners had made adverse findings. As of the writing of Byrnes' letter, 79 had been removed, leaving 205 (Evans, *Blacklisted*, 179-193).

It is indeed strange that whether the number of Communist spies in the State Department was 57 or 205 should become the more important issue, rather than that there were any spies at all. As Ann Coulter put it in an article in *Human Events*, "Having only 57 Communists in the State Department was apparently considered a great success for a Democratic administration" (Coulter 15).

While the speech had been broadcast over the radio, and even taped, it appears that the radio station erased the tape before the numbers controversy erupted (it being the common practice for radio stations not to save tapes of programs). The local newspaper, the *Wheeling Intelligencer*, ran an article by reporter Frank Desmond, in which Desmond reported that McCarthy had said 205, rather than 57. McCarthy had given Desmond a rough draft of his speech in which the higher number of 205 appeared, and Desmond simply used that number in his article (Evans 180).

McCarthy had also given rough draft copies to two other individuals, as well, but stressed to them that he would be revising his speech before its delivery. Desmond later conceded that the 205 quotation was taken from the rough draft of the speech, and not actually from what McCarthy said in his talk (Evans 182). The other two men who had been given rough drafts also testified that McCarthy did not simply read his speech, but rather spoke extemporaneously. Had McCarthy actually read his speech verbatim, Evans noted, the audience would have heard outlandish statements such as the Soviet Union controlled 80 *billion* people, and no one recalled such a thing (Evans 183).

Evans tracked down three attendees in 2000, shortly after the 50th anniversary of the Wheeling speech. All three agreed that McCarthy was clearly not simply reading a speech. The most detailed memory of the event came from Eva Lou Ingersoll, who insisted that McCarthy's 57 number was the correct number. According to Evans' recollection of the interview, Mrs. Ingersoll consulted notes she had taken on her phone bill after the numbers controversy erupted. She had written 205, and then she wrote "57 cc." The first figure she recalled as referring to a number being investigated, while the 57 referred to "card-carrying" members of the Communist Party (Evans 185).

Instead of concern over 57 Communist Party members, loyal to the Soviet Union, working inside the U.S. Department of State, the Truman Administration and its defenders circled the wagons, and made McCarthy the issue. Many insisted that McCarthy reveal the names of the Communists on his list, but McCarthy refused. His goal was not to unfairly announce the names to the general public (and possibly smear truly innocent individuals), but rather to move the Truman Administration to take action.

Of course, the only "action" taken by the Truman Administration and its Democratic Party defenders was to attack McCarthy, play a numbers game, and put forth the impression that McCarthy had been caught "changing the story."

Why did the Democrats attack McCarthy instead of sharing his concern about subversives inside the government? Arthur Herman contended that it was a defensive political strategy. "In many ways, the vehemence of the Democrats' attacks against McCarthy for the next several months stemmed from a mixture of frustration, after having been so badly fooled in the Hiss case, and fear. If the Democrats couldn't undo the damage from the previous fiasco, they could at least direct all their anger at this ill-mannered political novice and prevent another" (102).

Exactly how many Soviet spies permeated the U.S. government is, of course, unknown, but scholars examining the KGB files have concluded that it was immense. According to Herman, Allan Weinstein and

Alexander Vassiliev went through the KGB files and compiled a list of classified materials taken by Soviet spies, and it "ran to over 150 single-spaced pages." And that probably only represented a fraction of the total (106).

Of all the individuals supposedly smeared by McCarthy, perhaps none was more sympathetically cast than Annie Lee Moss, an Army Signal Corps employee. Mrs. Moss had been a listed member of the Communist Party until 1945, when she obtained a job in the Signal Corps cafeteria. Later, she was moved into a position in the Pentagon coding room. An FBI informant, Mary Markward, alerted Roy Cohn about Mrs. Moss. Markward had infiltrated the Communist Party, and swore to having seen Moss' name and address on a list of Communist Party members in the Washington, D.C. area (Cohn 121-123; Herman 334).

Moss' job allowed her access to classified material, but the Army argued that she was merely a relay machine operator. She was called to appear before McCarthy's Senate committee in March, 1954. It was known that she had been suspended from her job as a result of the charges against her, and she was now unemployed. While many who came before McCarthy's committee opted to "take the 5th," Moss did not, and denied her membership in the Party, although simply being a member of the Communist Party was not a crime. She even answered, "Who's that?" when she was asked if she had ever heard of Karl Marx, effecting a look of puzzlement (Herman 335).

Moss offered that perhaps this could all just be a case of mistaken identity. "I know there are three Annie Lee Mosses living in the area," and she speculated that could be the reason that copies of the *Daily Worker* were delivered to her 72 R Street address. Moss said she would soon be reduced to welfare because of her job loss (Herman 335).

Democrat Senator Stuart Symington offered to get her a new job, to an explosion of applause. After Edward R. Murrow's *See It Now* program featured Moss as a pathetically abused African-American woman facing the tyranny of Senator Joseph McCarthy, phone calls and telegrams ran almost nine-to-one in support of Moss (Herman 335).

Evans' contention is that Moss was prepped by Symington before her appearance, citing the transcript for evidence. Symington asked Moss, "Do you know anybody else in this town named Moss? Have you ever looked up a telephone number—-are there any Mosses in Washington besides you?" (Evans 530).

To which Moss replied, "Yes, sir, there are three Annie Lee Mosses."

Senator Henry Jackson even asked her to repeat that statement.

Perhaps no single episode caused McCarthy and his aide Roy Cohn to look worse than this supposed case of mistaken identity, smearing an "innocent" person, and costing a poor, hard-working Black woman her job at the Pentagon.

In 1958, the Subversive Activities Control Board issued a report on the case of Annie Lee Moss. The report stated, without equivocation, that the Annie Lee Moss who took the witness stand that day in 1954, and answered, "Who's that?" to a question about Karl Marx, and denied having ever been a member of the Communist Party, was indeed the same Annie Lee Moss that had been a member of the Communist Party in the 1940s (Herman 336).

There were not three Annie Lee Mosses in D.C., but only one. The one who perjured herself before a Senate committee that she had never been a member of the Communist Party. The three Mosses listed in the phone book included Anna Lee Moss, Annie Moss, and the Communist Annie Lee Moss (Evans 539).

Sadly, far too many get all the history they wish to get from the motion picture screen, put out by leftist actors, producers, directors, and writers. Once someone has seen history on the Big Screen, it is very difficult to persuade them otherwise. You can tell them that Joe McCarthy never took a mop and swung it at doctors and nurses in the hospital, but they know what they saw, in a TV movie. A more recent movie even glamorized Annie Lee Moss: George Clooney's *Good Night and Good Luck*, released in 2005. While it is somewhat understandable that some could have been taken in by Annie Lee Moss in 1954, Clooney's propaganda movie appeared almost 50 years after the report of the Subversive Activities Control Board, conclusively proving that Annie Lee Moss was not only a Communist, but that she had lied about it under oath to a committee of the U.S. Senate (Evans 538).

Clooney even admitted later that he knew that Moss was a Communist. But those who saw his movie were not told that.

So, the next time you hear that Joseph McCarthy smeared "innocent" people, or created the Hollywood Blacklist, or chaired the House Committee on Un-American Activities, or "changed his story" about the number of Reds in the State Department, you will know that the person is either lying, or is just ignorant of the facts.

Even if a conservative uses the term McCarthyism, as in McCarthyism of the Left. There cannot be any McCarthyism of the Left, because there was never any McCarthyism of the Right, if it is defined as "smearing innocent people."

The person most smeared in the entire so-called McCarthy Era was Senator Joseph Raymond McCarthy.

LIBEL #7

CLARENCE THOMAS SEXUALLY HARASSED ANITA HILL

"I cannot imagine anything that I said or did to Anita Hill that could have been mistaken for sexual harassment . . . I have not done what she has alleged, and I still do not know what I could have possibly done to cause her to make these allegations," Clarence Thomas told the Senate Judiciary Committee, in an emotionally-charged response to the accusation from Anita Hill, that Thomas had repeatedly sexually harassed her during her tenure at the Department of Education and the Equal Employment Opportunity Commission (EEOC), while Thomas was boss (Danforth 132).

A large television audience watched as Thomas responded to last-minute charges by an obscure law professor at the University of Oklahoma threatened to undo his nomination to the U.S. Supreme Court. "When I stood next to the president in Kennebunkport, being nominated to the Supreme Court of the United States, that was a high honor. But as I sit here, before you, 103 days later, that honor has been crushed. From the very beginning charges were leveled against me from the shadows—charges of drug abuse, anti-Semitism, wife-beating, drug use by family members, that I was a quota appointment, confirmation conversion and much, much more, and now, this.

I have complied with the rules. I responded to a document request that produced over 30,000 pages of documentation. And I have testified for five full days, under oath. I have endured this ordeal for 103 days. Reporters sneaking into my garage to examine books I read. Reporters and interest groups swarming over divorce papers, looking for dirt. Unnamed people starting preposterous and damaging rumors. Calls all over the country specifically requesting dirt. This is not American. This is Kafkaesque. It has got to stop. It must stop for the benefit of future nominees, and our country. Enough is enough" (Danforth 133).

Following the testimony of Hill, which followed Thomas' powerful testimony, in which Hill described a man obsessed with pornography,

Thomas returned to rebut her explicit testimony. Hill testified that Thomas had subjected her to stories of a character in a porn movie named Long Dong Silver, and asking her one time how a pubic hair had gotten on his Coke can. Ironically, as her charges became increasingly specific, as vile as they were, it reinforced in Thomas' mind the assurance that he had done no wrong to Hill. As his friend and mentor, Senator John Danforth recalled in his book, *Resurrection: The Confirmation of Clarence Thomas*, "Now there could be no room to suppose that he had said something or done something that was innocently intended but misconstrued. This could not be a question of mistake. This was plainly wrong" (Danforth 138).

Thomas was blunt in his rebuttal. "I would like to start by saying unequivocally, uncategorically [sic] that I deny each and every single allegation against me today that suggested in any way that I had conversations of a sexual nature or about pornographic material with Anita Hill, that I ever attempted to date her, that I ever had any personal sexual interest in her, or that I in any way ever harassed her.

Second, and I think a more important point, I think this today is a travesty. I think that it is disgusting. I think that this hearing should never occur in America. This is a case in which this sleaze, this dirt was searched for by staffers of members of this committee, was then leaked to the media, and this committee and this body validated it and displayed it in prime time over our entire nation" (Danforth 148).

After asking if any member of the committee would like this sort of sleaze said about them, Thomas summed up his feelings about the whole confirmation process, and how it had been handled. "The Supreme Court is not worth it. No job is worth it. I am not here for that. I am here for my name, my family, my life and my integrity. I think something is dreadfully wrong with this country, when any person, any person in this free country would be subjected to this" (Danforth 148).

Asserting that the FBI investigation had turned up nothing to justify serious consideration of the accusations, Thomas concluded. "This is a circus. This is a national disgrace. And from my standpoint, as a black American, as far as I am concerned, it is a high-tech lynching for uppity blacks who in any way think for themselves, to do for themselves, to have different ideas, and it is a message that, unless you kow-tow to an old order, this is what will happen to you, you will be lynched, destroyed, caricatured by a committee of the U.S. Senate, rather than hung from a tree" (Danforth 148).

Combined with powerful testimony from former employees of Thomas, who directly refuted Hill's case, the hearings concluded with a dramatic swing in Thomas' favor in the court of public opinion. His confirmation by the U.S. Senate was a result of this change of opinion. At the close of the hearing, about two-third of Americans polled thought Thomas, not Hill, was telling the truth. By the end of 1992, however, the *Washington Post* reported that the public now believed Hill, 53%-37% (Danforth 200).

This is instructive. Once Thomas was confirmed, conservatives largely believed the battle was over. But not liberals. They understand far better than conservatives the importance of winning every historical incident, in the court of public opinion. They never concede. Conservatives can never be allowed to "win" a battle in this arena. Using their advantages in the liberal media, the liberal forces that dominate the popular culture, and liberals in academia, they are allowed to change, even distort, public perceptions of historical events, with hardly any resistance from conservatives.

As George Orwell wrote in his class dystopian novel, *1984*, those who control the past can control the future. This is exactly what the character assassination of Clarence Thomas was all about. As a prominent black conservative, Thomas could be expected to emerge as a significant role model for those in the African-American community. That simply could not be allowed. While keeping Thomas off the Supreme Court was certainly an important goal for those on the Left, it was just as important to so destroy this man's reputation that he could never be held up as a role model by the Right.

This is why it is important to challenge the false versions of events created on the Left about the Thomas case, and in the other great libels of history. Every time, these distortions of history have an underlying political purpose, which is to advance the liberal version of events, so as to control present and future political and social struggles.

With this in mind, let us look at what actually happened in the case of the ugly accusations by Anita Hill made against Clarence Thomas.

After Ronald Reagan was elected president in 1980, one of the individuals hired by the incoming conservative presidential administration was Thomas. Thomas had graduated from Yale Law School, and had drifted into a more politically and socially conservative viewpoint since his earlier somewhat "radical" days. Not surprisingly, the Reagan Administration had a political self-interest in bringing more conservative blacks on board. And, as the Thomas confirmation hearings demonstrated, the Left had opposite political motives to prevent the creation of such conservative black role models.

Thomas was appointed to head up the Civil Rights division of the Department of Education, a department that Reagan had actually targeted for abolition during his campaign. But with the House of Representatives still firmly in control of the Democratic Party, that was unlikely to happen. "Shortly after I started work," Thomas recalled in his autobiography, *My Grandfather's Son*, "Gil Hardy called me and asked me to 'help a sister' who was leaving his firm." Hardy, who died in 1989, had been one of Thomas' closest friends. A black lawyer, Hardy was a partner in the Washington law firm of Wald, Harkrader, and Ross (Clarence Thomas 140).

The 'sister' in question was Anita Hill. Thomas asked Hardy if Hill was a Republican, and when told that she was not, Thomas told Hardy it would be "all but impossible to shepherd a political appointee through the vetting process unless the person had been a longtime Reagan supporter." But since Hardy was such a close friend, Thomas consented to interview Hill. In the interview, he asked her why a Yale Law School graduate would want to leave a prestigious law firm to come to work for an obscure civil-rights agency. Hill told Thomas that her "options were limited" because her boss would not give her a recommendation. According to Hill, the partner had asked her for a date, and when she declined, he began giving her bad work assignments and performance assessments (Clarence Thomas 140).

Shifting topics, Thomas asked Hill her opinion of President Reagan. "I detest him," Hill said flatly. Knowing he could not hire her as a political appointee, but recalling how difficult it was to find work himself after graduation, he gave her a job as a non-political employee instead. Thomas described her work as not outstanding, but "adequate" (Clarence Thomas 140).

The next year, Reagan asked Thomas to take over the Equal Employment Opportunity Commission (EEOC). Thomas called his staff together, and announced that he would be leaving the Department of Education, and going to the EEOC. Anita Hill immediately told Thomas that she wished to follow him to EEOC. Thomas told her that he would consider it, but that she had a "safe" job at Education, thanks to a new collective-bargaining agreement that assured career lawyers like Hill had the same protections as career civil servants.

Hill, however, was persistent. "You're a rising star," she replied. "I want to go with you" (Clarence Thomas 150).

Thomas' interim secretary at EEOC, Anna Jenkins, was pestered by Hill and Gil Hardy to hire Hill, and Thomas reluctantly agreed. She immediately claimed the largest office in the suite. Because Hill had no experience with employment law, Thomas asked two young career employees, Allyson Duncan and Bill Ng, to join his personal staff (Clarence Thomas 156).

Near the end of 1982, Chris Roggerson, Thomas' chief of staff, told him that Hill was not performing up to expectations and was failing to finish her assignments on time. "It had been bothering me as well that she [Anita Hill] seemed far too interested in my social calendar. She regularly inquired about my after-hours activities and on more than one occasion had asked if she could accompany me to professional functions" (Clarence Thomas 171-172).

Then, in early 1983, Roggerson took a job in California, creating a need for Thomas to hire a new chief of staff. Hill approached Thomas about the job, telling him that she "deserved it," because of her degree from Yale Law School, adding that Allyson Duncan had only gone to Duke and Bill Ng was just a graduate from Boston College. "It would have been hard for her to come up with an argument less likely to sway me," Thomas recalled (172).

When Thomas picked Allyson for the post, Hill stormed into Thomas' office, and accused him of favoring lighter-skinned women. Duncan was a lighter-skinned black woman, and Thomas was dating a lighter-skinned black woman at the time. Thomas told her that he found her accusation, attitude, and reason "equally irritating." Hill vowed to look for another job, and stormed out of his office (172).

Hill made similar comments about Thomas' "preference" for light-skinned women to Armstrong Williams. Hill had discovered that Thomas was dating a racially mixed woman, and made a negative comment about it, but finally concluded, "Well, at least he's not dating a white woman." Of course, Thomas eventually *did* marry a white woman (Brock 360).

Soon after this incident, Elaine Jenkins, a well-known Republican, whose husband Howard was the only black member of the National Labor Relations Board, asked Thomas to speak at an EEO luncheon at Oral Roberts University Law School in Tulsa, Oklahoma. Thomas thought it would be a good opportunity for Hill, who was from Oklahoma. He reasoned that she could spend some time with her family, and consider her options. When he suggested this to her, she readily agreed, and flew out a few days before the seminar (Clarence Thomas 173). According to Hill, Bill Ng also went (Hill 79). Thomas took an early morning flight the day of the luncheon and returned home the same day (Clarence Thomas 173).

In her book, *Speaking Truth to Power*, Hill tells a different version, writing that she and Thomas rode *on the same plane to Oklahoma*. According to Hill, "I still recall that on that fateful trip to Oklahoma Thomas had wanted me to sit with him in the rear of the airplane. I told him that I preferred to sit up front because the smoking allowed in the rear in those days bothered my allergies" (Hill 80). It is hard to imagine that Thomas said anything at all to her on the flight, if he was not even on the plane.

Upon arrival at the seminar, Thomas was introduced to Charles Kothe, the dean of the law school. Dean Kothe told Thomas that Hill had performed well at the seminar, and asked Thomas for permission to speak with her about joining the faculty. Thomas told Kothe that Hill was, in fact, looking for a job, and had family in Oklahoma. He added that Hill had not performed well at EEOC, but offered that she would probably do better as she matured. Kothe offered Hill a faculty position, which she accepted (Clarence Thomas 173). In Hill's version, she wrote, "Almost by chance, I was asked to interview for a position at the O.W. Coburn School of Law at Oral Roberts University in Tulsa" (Hill 79).

Reviewing these two accounts, it would appear that Hill and Thomas could *not* have been on the same plane, since Thomas arrived later, and was then told by the Dean that Hill had "performed well" at the seminar. This contradiction, in and of itself, is not earth-shattering, but it does indicate that Hill recalled the event in such a way as to advance her version of the relationship she had with Thomas.

In her book, Hill expressed some concern about the "conservative ideology" of the school (80).

The EEOC staff refused to throw a farewell party for Hill. Armstrong Williams, an employee at EEOC, and a politically conservative black man, like Thomas, had warned Thomas that Hill was Thomas' "mortal enemy, and will do everything to destroy you" (Danforth 38-39).

Three years later, Hill contacted Thomas and asked him to speak at an EEO function in Tulsa. Thomas shared one of the head tables with Hill and Kothe (who by that time was working for Thomas at EEOC), and Kothe's wife. Kothe had planned to drive Thomas to the airport the next morning, but Hill showed up for breakfast and insisted on driving Thomas in her new Peugeot. "She was excited about the car and seemed happy . . . She called me from time to time after that, but so far as I can remember, I never saw her again" (Andrew Thomas 380).

Hill does not mention volunteering to take Thomas to the airport in her new Peugeot, in her book.

While Thomas said he thought Hill was "happy" at ORU, she tells a slightly different story in her book. She contended that she posed a "ideological and conceptual problem" for some of the students. "I am certain that, as a black woman, I challenged their notion of authority." She wrote that a group of "male students protested my assignment to teach commercial law on the basis that I was unqualified to do so." She argued in her book that the reason for their resistance to her was because of the "conservative racial and gender politics and even prejudices of many in the student body" which "went a long way to convince them that I did not belong in front of the class in the role of their instructor" (85).

Hill continued to call Thomas, "almost always when she wanted something," Thomas remembered. She usually spoke with Diane Holt, Thomas's secretary, and left messages, and even called Thomas at his home on occasion, until Thomas changed his phone number. (Thomas said he did not change the number because of Hill, but rather because he had moved). The only important call that Thomas said he could remember was in 1985. Oral Roberts University had moved its law school to Regent University, a Christian school in Virginia, and Hill called Thomas to encourage Thomas to hire Dean Kothe. She told Thomas that Kothe had helped her get a new job at the University of Oklahoma College of Law. Thomas did hire Kothe as a legal counsel at EEOC, and was very pleased with his performance (Clarence Thomas 179).

Finally, in 1991, after Thomas had been on the Court of Appeals in the District of Columbia for a couple of years, President George Herbert Walker Bush nominated Thomas to a vacant seat on the United States Supreme Court. As with the powerful assault that had sunk the nomination of Judge Robert Bork during the days of the Reagan Administration in 1987, liberal forces made a strong effort to defeat Thomas. Thomas used what has been called a "rope a dope strategy" (named after its use by Muhammad Ali in his upset victory over heavyweight boxing champion George Foreman), in which Thomas basically played defense, cautiously answering questions from the Democrat majority on the Senate Judiciary Committee. It appeared that Thomas would be confirmed, with estimates that he would receive in excess of 60 votes, despite the Democratic Party control of the Senate.

Then, Thomas received a call that two agents of the Federal Bureau of Investigation (FBI) needed to come by and speak with him. Thomas wondered what possible reason the FBI would need to interview him, but as he recalled in his biography, "I feared the worst."

When Thomas' nomination was announced, one of Hill's friends from law school, Susan Hoerchner, a workers' compensation in California, thought of Hill. She seemed to recall that Hill had told her, around the time Hill began working at the Department of Education, that her boss had pressured her to date him. Hoerchner contacted Hill at her home in Norman, Oklahoma, inquiring if Hill was going to go public with charges of "sexual harassment" against Thomas. When Hill did not give a direct answer, Hoerchner asked Hill if she could tell "story" to others, and Hill consented (Andrew Thomas 377-379).

Through the rumor mill, the story eventually made its way to the staff of liberal Democrat Senator Howard Metzenbaum, a member of the Judiciary

Committee. Another staffer for Senator Edward Kennedy, also a member of the committee, joined the Metzenbaum staffer in a separate investigation. Finally, James Brudney, an attorney on Metzenbaum's staff and a friend of Hill's at Yale, began discussing the issue with Hill and others.

Hill told Brudney that she did not want her accusations made public. Brudney told her this was an opportunity to "ruin" Thomas, and sink his nomination. He told her that they could possibly even get Thomas to withdraw, without a public airing of the charges. Hill called Harriet Grant, the nominations counsel to the committee, and told her that she wished to make an anonymous allegation, and let the committee investigate the matter. Committee Chairman Joe Biden refused, saying Hill would not be allowed to remain anonymous in order for the charges to be pursued (Andrew Thomas 372-272).

As the hearings neared their conclusion, Hill contacted Grant again, and told her that she was now willing to give up her anonymity. Hill was told that her charges would be turned over to the FBI for further investigation. Hill hesitated, but after some fellow law professors at OU encouraged her to push forward, she finally agreed to type out a four page statement. Although the statement began with the words, "I swear," she neglected to have the paper notarized. She then faxed the statement to the committee.

As a result, FBI agents came to visit Anita Hill—-and Clarence Thomas.

"There's an allegation of sexual harassment," the male agent said, according to Andew Peyton Thomas (no relation), in his biography of Thomas, *Clarence Thomas*. He told Thomas that the accuser was Anita Hill (380).

Thomas found the accusations incredible. "I could have cried," Thomas recalled. He told them that he had been dating another woman at the time of the alleged harassment, that he had helped Hill get her job at the ORU Law School, and mentioned her volunteering to drive him to the airport after the second ORU seminar.

Thomas told a friend shortly after the two FBI agents left that "this is the ultimate way to destroy" a single black man. "It's a smear job that you can't get off," Thomas told the friend, who recalled that there was "never a waver" in Thomas' response that the allegations were false.

When the Hill accusations went public, Thomas' confirmation went from probable to very much in doubt. At first, the Republicans wanted to push forward with the floor vote, but when it became apparent that Thomas would lose, due to the Hill allegations, they agreed to a delay in order to have hearings on her charges.

Ironically, a *Washington Post* article revealed that Hill had been briefly considered as a witness *for* Thomas, but had been removed from consideration when she publicly criticized Thomas for lacking "sympathy" for his own sister, who was on welfare (Danforth 19). Hill said of Thomas, "He doesn't relate to people who don't make it on their own." Thomas told a group of Republicans that his sister gets mad when the mailman is late with her welfare check (Hill 100). Now, Hill would testify in an effort to scuttle Thomas' hopes for a place on the Supreme Court.

Thomas and his defenders attempted to make sense of this last-minute effort to defeat him by ruining his reputation. Thomas recalled that Gil Hardy, when he was asking Thomas to hire Hill at the Department of Education, told Thomas that Hill was being mistreated by a partner after she refused to date him. Diane Holt, Thomas' secretary at both Education and the EEOC, also recalled the story of Hill claiming she left the law firm because of sexual harassment. Interestingly, Susan Hoerchner, who initially contacted Hill about Thomas' alleged acts of harassment at Education, had placed the time of her recollection of Hill's "harassment" story as *before* she went to work for Thomas in August, 1981, and at the time she was employed at Wald, Harkrader, and Ross. Because of his close friendship with Hardy, and despite her clear anti-Reagan views ("She was very critical of the president," Thomas recalled), Thomas hired her on as a Schedule A attorney. Schedule A lawyers are career employees, and her job was not dependent upon her political viewpoint, as would be the case with Schedule C employees (Danforth 36).

Thomas told Larry Silberman, a fellow appeals court judge that he was never attracted to Hill, and that "she had bad breath" (Danforth 37). For her part, in her book, Hill wrote, "I was not attracted to him" (Hill 68).

Diane Holt recalled Hill as a liberal feminist, describing her as acting like a "spoiled brat," who always wanted her own way (Danforth 37).

Hill explained to the committee why she followed Thomas from the Department of Education to EEOC. She said that she was fearful that Reagan was going to abolish the department, and that she might lose her job there. Thomas disputed that contention as "nonsense." Even if the department was abolished, the Office of Civil Rights in which she worked had its own budget, and it was going to continue (Danforth 37).

Years before, Thomas had worked in the office of Senator John Danforth of Missouri and they had remained good friends. Danforth was livid at the last-minute smear job. "First, this was a last-ditch attempt to defeat a nomination that we had thought we had won. The Hill story was identical to the weekend-before-the-election attacks made by losing candidates against winning candidates. Just as last-minute political attacks should be dismissed by the voters, so this last minute attack should be dismissed by the American people" (Danforth 60).

Mark Pooletta, a young lawyer in the White House counsel's office, was assigned to work for Thomas' confirmation. After the Hill allegations went public, Pooletta contacted 20-25 women from the EEOC staff. *All* were shocked and 17 were willing to either file affidavits or testify on Thomas' behalf (Danforth 64-65).

Diane Holt had recalled five or six calls to Thomas from Hill *after* Hill had left the EEOC, but as it turned out, they found telephone logs for *eleven* phone calls from Hill. This would not include times in which Thomas was available, and Holt put her on through. One phone call from Hill left the hotel room number where she was staying in D.C. (Danforth 66).

During her testimony, Hill claimed that Thomas harassed her with stories of a porn scene involving a black man known as Long Dong Silver. However, when Hill taught at Oral Roberts University, she taught discrimination law, and Long Dong Silver was a case discussed in the field of employment discrimination. As Danforth recalled in his book, "(A) sexual harassment case from the same judicial circuit in which Anita Hill resided involved a man who had made reference to Long Dong Silver" (Danforth 152-153).

After the testimonies of Hill and Thomas were concluded, several women who had worked for Thomas delivered their testimony. Janet

Brown told the committee that she had been sexually harassed in the workplace years earlier, and she found the experience "humiliating." She then expressed astonishment at the Hill accusations against Thomas. "Let me assure you that the last thing I would ever have done is follow the man who did this to a new job, call him on the phone or voluntarily share the same air space again." She said that Thomas had helped her through the "pain" of that experience (Danforth 184). Hill does not mention Brown in her book.

Nancy Altman described herself as a pro-choice feminist, who cared deeply about women's issues. She told the committee that she shared an office with Thomas for "two years," adding that "our desks were a few feet apart. Because we worked in such close quarters, I could hear virtually every conversation for two years that Clarence Thomas had. Not once in those two years did I ever hear Clarence Thomas make a sexist or an offensive comment, not once." Adding "This is wrong," Altman told the committee, "(W)hen sexual harassment occurs, other women in the workplace know about it" (Danforth 184-185). Hill does not mention Altman in her book.

Lori Saxon worked with both Hill and Thomas at the Department of Education. "My office was just down the hall from Anita Hill's during her tenure at the Department of Education. I never saw any harassment go on in the office. The office was run very professionally. Clarence Thomas and Anita Hill were always very cordial and friendly in their relations. There was never any evidence of any harassment toward any of the female employees. I dealt with Anita Hill on daily basis in performing my duties. She was happy in her position and she liked working for Clarence Thomas" (Danforth 185). Lori Saxon is not mentioned by Hill in her book.

Anna Jenkins, who had worked at EEOC, told the committee that she had "daily contact" with both Hill and Thomas. "Judge Thomas' conduct around me, Anita Hill, and other staffers was always proper and professional. I have never witnessed Judge Thomas say anything or do anything that could be construed as sexual harassment. I never witnessed him making sexual advances toward any female, nor have I witnessed him engaging in sexually oriented conversations with women." Jenkins added that she never saw any strained relationship between Thomas and Hill (Danforth 185-186). Hill does not mention Jenkins in her book.

Even Hill herself had once told Armstrong Williams that Thomas was "the ideal boss," and compared him favorably to men that she had worked with before who had less respect for women. Not surprisingly, this is not the testimony she offered at the hearings, nor does she dispute Williams' account of their conversation in her book.

Despite overwhelming evidence in Thomas' favor, the Left has succeeded in creating a false narrative that Thomas did, in fact, sexually harass Anita Hill, and got away with it, and now sits on the Supreme Court. Senator Danforth explained how it was done. "The stain was spread with the help of the media, and it reached the members of the Judiciary Committee, especially those who had supported Clarence. Liberal columnists portrayed the questioning of Anita Hill as abusive and television shows lampooned both Clarence and the committee. Oliver Stone amended the script of his docudrama *JFK* to add Arlen Specter's name to the assertion that an obscure but ambitious junior counselor when the Kennedy assassination was investigated was a liar. The film was released during Arlen's reelection campaign, and the inserted mention of his name was the cause of boos and hisses in movie theaters" (200-201).

David Brock wrote a best-seller, *The Real Anita Hill*, which carefully challenged the Hill charges, and found them wanting. His book was given a very negative treatment in the media, including such unusual methods as scheduling an Anita Hill defender to appear with him simultaneously when the book was reviewed. Katie Couric accused Brock of having "conservative biases." The *New Yorker* turned the review of his book over to Jane Mayer and Jill Abramson, who were writing a book in defense of Hill. A bookstore owner quoted in the *New York Times* compared his book to *Mein Kampf* (Brock 395-400). Hill said of Brock, "As a white male he is given permission to define me, a black woman, on whatever terms he chooses . . . He is presumed to be free of bias, no matter how obviously biased his work may be" (Hill 282).

In her book, Hill said she left OU Law School because of "discrimination," to take a job in Women's Studies at Brandeis University. She dismissed accusations from law students at ORU, who complained of her being unprepared for class, as racists. In her book, she gave an explanation as to why she continued contact with Thomas. "I began to bifurcate my feelings about Clarence Thomas psychologically. I was able to think of him as a former employer and even a personal acquaintance with whom I could continue a congenial relationship . . . My sense of professionalism, which some describe as opportunism, allowed me to divorce my personal feelings from my work interests." She argued that she "refused to let his bad behavior cheat me of every benefit of my good work" (Hill 83). In her Senate testimony, she claimed she did use her relationship with Thomas for her own professional advantage (Andrew Thomas 540-542).

At one point in her testimony, she conceded that she "might have" discussed Thomas' possible withdrawal without her testifying, and then later admitted that it was in fact discussed, not just might have been discussed (Andrew Thomas 542).

While the Left rallied to Hill's cause, arguing that a woman should always be believed in any charge of sexual harassment, regardless of the evidence, they radically changed their stance with the Clinton Scandals of 1998, only seven years later. Betty Friedan dismissed President Bush as Public Enemy No. 1 for his support of Thomas over Hill, but defended President Clinton over three women who charged him with sexual harassment—-Paula Jones, Kathleen Willey, and Juanita Broaddrick (who actually said that Clinton raped her). In a classic example of double-standard hypocrisy, the National Organization for Women fought against Thomas, but strongly defended Clinton.

The 26 senators who had voted *against* Thomas' confirmation and were still in office in 1998, voted to keep Clinton in office. Every single one (Andrew Thomas 554).

And even Anita Hill herself defended Clinton. In a *Newsweek* article, Hill said the two situations "are quite different." In an appearance on *Meet the Press*, Hill supported the defense of Clinton by feminist leaders, the same ones who had attacked Thomas. "We live in a political world, and the reality is that there are larger issues other than just individual behavior" (Andrew Thomas 553-554).

"I was torn," Hill wrote in her book, "because Ms. Jones was aligned with people who were Bill Clinton's political enemies," admitting that

"Paula Jones' claim that Bill Clinton sexually harassed her tests our commitments to this issue" (302).

This attitude explains what occurred in the Hill attack upon Thomas, and her defense by the Liberal Establishment. It is the modern incarnation of Plato's *noble lie*. If the cause is just, and a lie will advance that just cause, then a lie becomes moral. At least that is the view of far too many on the Left.

Sadly, many who are victims of historical libel by the Left remain undefended because many conservatives are busy fighting *today's* ideological battles. What they do not fully realize is that many of today's ideological battles are won by the Left because the Right just allows the Left to win by default in what is a case of unilateral disarmament.

Hill wrote, "Each case must be examined on its own, with motivation and credibility taken into full account" (302). In this case, taking into account motivation and credibility, I believe the evidence is on the side of Justice Thomas.

Clarence Thomas is an example of a good conservative who is a victim of this liberal revision of the historical record, and he should be defended, not left on the battlefield to fend for himself. This is not just for Thomas' benefit, but also for our own.

LIBEL #8

COLUMBUS WAS A MONSTER WHO DID NOTHING GOOD

When it comes to an historical analysis of Christopher Columbus, it is somewhat more difficult to address the libel against him, because the charges are so preposterous that one's first thought is, "Can anyone really believe this stuff?" But, Columbus, who was once hailed as one of the greatest men of all time, has fallen victim to 21st century political correctness, in which persons of European ancestry, especially those who are unabashedly Christian, are automatically considered suspect.

The libel(s) against Columbus generally go something like this: Columbus was a racist killer, who enslaved Indians, started the African slave trade, and even used captured Indians as dog food! James Loewen, a left-wing former college history professor, wrote in his book, *The Lies My Teacher Told Me*, that the pre-Columbian population of Haiti was eight million, but "When Christopher Columbus returned to Spain," the number of Indian adults was 1,100,000. Larry Schweikert, in his book, *48 Liberal Lies About American History*, "To think that any pre-modern civilization could eliminate seven million people in just over two years defies all logic, not to mention history." After all, he only had three ships on his first voyage, and even on his second voyage, he probably had no more than a thousand men, Schweikert contended, and asked how "one thousand men . . . could *kill seven million* people in three years!" (112-113).

When Marxist Hugo Chavez was the dictator of Venezuela, he even claimed that the Spanish and the Portuguese massacred South America's Indians at an average rate of "roughly one every 10 minutes" (Ardon).

Radical American Indian activist Russell Means expressed similar outrage, saying, "Columbus makes Hitler look like a juvenile delinquent. He was a racist, a mass murderer, a slave trader, a rapist, and a plunderer." George P. Horse Capture summed it up, "No sensible Indian person can celebrate the arrival of Columbus" (Grant 117).

Certainly not, if all the rapings, killings, and enslavement from 1492 until recent times can be considered the fault of Christopher Columbus.

But, of course, since Columbus died on May 20, 1506, it is highly unlikely that he was involved in much raping, killing, and enslaving *after* that time. George Grant writes, in his *The Last Crusader: The Untold Story of Christopher Columbus,* "To be sure there were perverse abuses . . . But heap all that upon the shoulders of one man—-a man who unleashed upon the Americans far more good than woe—-is patently absurd. Whatever ecocide is—-or if there really is such a vice—-Columbus was not guilty of it. Far from being a racist, he proved time after time to be overly enamored with the native populations he encountered on his travels. And the charge of slave-trading is merely malicious falsehood" (127)

In her 2011 book, *Columbus and the Quest for Jerusalem,* retired Stanford professor Carol Delaney addressed this issue directly, when she said that the "presentist" perspective holds Columbus responsible for "consequences he did not intend, expect, or endorse" (Delaney 236). "He surely did not intend to commit genocide, of which he has been accused" (237). Yet, today, Columbus is no longer a "flesh and blood" person, but has become a symbol of the evil European. This has led to the desecration of Columbus statues each Columbus Day, a reversal of the attitude toward the great admiral in the 19th century, when Delaney notes Columbus was proposed for canonization (xii).

This is not to say that Europeans in general, and Spaniards in particular, did not rape, pillage, and slaughter indigenous peoples in the western hemisphere. There is reason that the *Black Legend* of Spanish misdeeds toward the natives developed—-it is was not purely an English invention in a larger propaganda war. But, when Columbus arrived in the Americas, the native peoples were already busy enslaving their neighbors (Delaney 238). They did not have to be taught slavery, for it already existed. Some tribes in the New World were particularly brutal toward fellow Indian tribes. As Victor Davis Hanson estimated, the Aztecs killed around 20,000 *per year* in ritual sacrifices (Schweikert 209).

To a large extent, Columbus is hated for his greatest virtue, which is that he brought Christianity to the New World, quickly replacing the polytheistic religions practiced before 1492. To many, this is probably his greatest evil, although most of his detractors are not going to be that honest about it. As John Ardon, a Catholic priest, wrote, "We can identify his critics by their religious affiliation or ideology" (Ardon).

When Columbus first made landfall in the West, he named the island San Salvador, as he wished for the salvation of the natives, desiring their peaceful conversion to the "Holy Faith," by love rather than force (Delaney 92).

Columbus reasoned that his evangelistic task would be relatively easy, as he did not detect a religion to convert them from. "I believe that they would become good Christians very quickly" (Delaney 98). Columbus' Roman Catholic Church faced a difficult challenge converting the peoples of Europe in the early part of the Middle Ages, because many of the European tribes had already accepted an Arian form of Christianity, which denied the Catholic doctrine of the Trinity. That is why the conversion of King Clovis and the Franks was so important. Not having already been won over to a heretical form of the Christian faith, the Frankish tribe readily accepted Trinitarian Christianity. As the Franks grew in strength, their alliance with the Roman Catholic Church proved mutually beneficial in augmenting the strength of the other, eventually producing the Holy Roman Empire of Charlemagne. Columbus, a keen student of history, considered the Indians, like the Franks, "fertile ground" for a smooth conversion.

It was Columbus' most passionate hope for the indigenous peoples. He ordered his men to treat them "courteously," noting they were the "most gentle people." He told the rulers of Spain that he had "much hope in our Lord" that they would soon "all" become Christians (Delaney 105). This is a theme that is ubiquitous in Columbus' diary. Robert Fuson, who translated the diary, noted that Columbus expressed "nothing but love and admiration for the Indians" (Delaney 107). Columbus is now pictured in the popular culture as being concerned primarily for gold and spices, but this desire was part of his larger motivation. It was his desire to find enough wealth to finance a "crusade" to free the Holy Land from Islamic domination, and "conquer the Holy Sepulcher [Christ's empty tomb]; for this I urged Your Highnesses," Columbus told King Ferdinand and Queen Isabella of Spain, "to spend *all the profits* [emphasis added] from this enterprise on the conquest of Jerusalem" (Delaney, prologue).

The Muslims had conquered Constantinople not too many years earlier, completing their multigenerational conquest of the Christian world in the East, including the Byzantine Empire and the lands where Jesus had lived, died, and risen from the dead. Columbus, after careful study of the Old and New Testaments, along with some readings in the works of the historian Flavius Josephus, and the noted church "father" Augustine, had concluded that the city of Jerusalem needed to be in Christian hands before the Lord would return. Specifically, Columbus believed the biblical prophecies would dictate the reconstruction of the temple first (Delaney 190). And Columbus believed that his present mission was part of the overall plan of God to see this accomplished. While certainly the desire to reach the East by sailing west involved economics, Columbus did not set out from Spain to enslave American Indians, since he was ignorant of their very existence. After reading of the travels of the Venetian Marco Polo, Columbus desired to reach the Gran Khan, the Mongol ruler of China. The Chinese monarchs had expressed an interest in the Christian faith. Columbus planned to complete the conversion of China, then combine forces to drive the Muslims out of the Holy Land (Delaney xv).

Pre-Columbian America is pictured as a paradise by those who wish to denigrate Columbus. It was not. Before Columbus set foot in the Western Hemisphere, slavery was hoary with age, widely practiced by indigenous peoples upon other indigenous peoples. War was common among them, mainly in frequent land disputes. The conquest of Mexico by Hernando Cortes is among the most amazing stories in world history, but today it is usually reduced to some simplistic morality play, such as Cortes conquered the peace-loving Aztecs, and took their gold. In reality, the Aztec Empire was a brutal tyranny that rivaled anything seen in Europe before the days of Stalin and Hitler.

To the Aztecs, natural forces such as the sun, rain, wind, and fire were personified as gods, gods who must be satisfied with human blood, and lots of it. Aztec priests offered up human sacrifices in the thousands, usually drawn from the populations of other native peoples who were slaves, or had been taken in war. These black-robed priests chanted to their gods as they tore out the hearts of living victims, sometimes thousands a day. In 1487, at a time when Columbus was still begging for the financing of his historic voyage, 20,000 human beings were offered up in one day to the god of war and the sun, Huitzilopochtli. These Aztecs practiced cannibalism. The Spanish Conquistadores, inspired by Christian moral standards, put a stop to both practices. If Columbus can be blamed for injustices which occurred after his death, surely he can also be credited with putting an end to human sacrifice and cannibalism because of his introduction of the Christian religion into the New World.

The Caribs, a war-like tribe hated by other indigenous peoples Columbus met, practiced what he regarded as the "accursed vice" of sodomy, and they were cannibals who kept body parts in their huts, sort of like decorations. They even castrated captured boys, in order to fatten them up for meals. To keep the Caribs from continuing their raids on his friends, Columbus ordered their canoes destroyed, and freed some of their enslaved peoples (Delaney 130).

Another libel directed at Columbus is that he launched the African slave trade, but there is no evidence to support such a claim. He certainly did not introduce slavery into the New World, for it had already existed there for centuries. He did send a few captured Caribs to Spain as slaves, reasoning they had a better chance of converting to the religion of the Christ by getting them out of decadent environment they were in (Delaney 132). The principal reason that Columbus objected to wholesale baptisms of native peoples was not so he could enslave them with a clear conscience, but rather so as to better first instruct them in the Catholic faith (Delaney 82-83).

Spanish priest Bartolome de Las Casas is often credited with defending the rights of American Indians in the Spanish empire. To shame the Spanish for their mistreatment of the Indians, Las Casas often exaggerated the extent of the atrocities and the size of the indigenous population (Ardon).

Las Casas originally advocated enslavement of the Indians, and was denied the confessional because of it, but reversed his position about 1514. His writings were later used by the English to build the Black Legend.

One of Las Casas' writings which has been used to attack the reputation of Columbus is his use of ferocious dogs against the Indians. The way it is presented it is that Columbus used the natives as dog food. The reality is that the dogs were used in war against the Taino Indians (a branch of the Arawak), which is certainly gruesome, but one must ask if that is any worse than using a sword to lop off a man's head. War is bad. It is certainly not true that Columbus simply used Indian flesh to feed his dogs.

Samuel Eliot Morrison, author of *Christopher Columbus, Mariner*, explained how the Spaniards "wisely did not wait to be surrounded or overwhelmed, but took the offensive." Armed with primitive muskets, which "alarmed the Tainos more than it harmed them," the 200 foot soldiers had a mere 20 horses and 20 hounds. The use of the horses, and the "savage dogs" led to a complete victory. Morrison said that "in every instance the Europeans had native allies. It was the inability of Indians to unite" that contributed greatly to their defeat. After centuries of fighting each other, the natives had a difficult time focusing on the Spaniard as the common enemy (98).

This war was the result of the Santa Maria running aground in Haiti. Because there was not enough room for the men on another boat, Columbus directed the 39-man crew to start a colony. A year later, Columbus discovered that the Indians had killed all of these men. This resulted in a war in which Columbus emerged victorious. The 500 Indians he captured and took to Spain were prisoners, not slaves. They were later released (De Seno). But Columbus did not start this war. When he left behind the settlement (which he called Navidad), the men quickly took to fighting among themselves, conducting raiding parties among the Indians, stealing the natives' goods. They raped women and kidnapped some as concubines. This naturally led to retaliation, in which the Indians understandably killed the men and burned their villages (Delaney 132).

Had the men followed his orders, peace may very well have continued. His instructions to the men of Navidad when he left was to do no harm to the Indians, and to respect their chief, Guananagari. He also directed them to stay together, "not to scatter," and not to "enter inland." Anticipating their temptations, Columbus ordered them to "avoid doing injury or using violence to the women, by with they could cause scandal and set a bad example." He pleaded with the men to "strive . . . by their soft and honest speech" to gain the good will of the Indians, "keeping their friendship and love" (Delaney 109).

Of course, the men ignored Columbus' wise counsel, and suffered the consequences, leading to war. Still, Columbus made efforts to reconcile with the natives, but the Europeans who sailed with him "resented his trust and seeming support of the Indians," who desired "revenge," rather than reconciliation (Delaney 134).

Las Casas, who is often cited as the source of much of Columbus' alleged cruelties, actually was highly complimentary of him in his *Historia de las Indias*. "He [Columbus] was a gentle man of great force and spirit, of lofty thoughts and naturally inclined to undertake worthy deeds and signal enterprises; patient and longsuffering, a forgiver of injustices who wished no more than that those who offended him should recognize their errors, and that the delinquents be reconciled to him; most constant and endowed with forbearance in the hardships and adversities which were always occurring and which were incredible and infinite; ever holding great confidence in divine providence" (De Seno).

Perhaps the most serious libel leveled against Columbus is that he committed genocide, and it is true that hundreds of thousands, perhaps millions, of native peoples died in the decades after the Spanish invasion. This charge is also the most easily refuted. The greatest cause of the deaths of the indigenous peoples of the western hemisphere was disease, as the Spaniards introduced smallpox, plague, and measles into North and South America.

"It is wrong also wrong to blame Columbus for bringing genocidal microbes to kill native Americans," Tommy De Sano wrote in, "The Truth About Christopher Columbus." De Seno noted that Columbus' detractors "make fun of him thinking he was in the East. So was his evil plan to bring disease to wipe out the East?" (De Seno).

As De Seno rightly contended, transcontinental contamination was going to happen at some point. And, it went both ways. While not nearly as widespread a killer as smallpox was to the Indians, syphilis was introduced into Europe from the Americas, and killed more than five million people.

The genesis of the attacks upon Columbus' reputation can be traced largely to his success. As John Ardon said, "Envy dogged his steps from the moment he set foot" in the America on October 12, 1492.

Advisors to the rulers in Spain had argued strongly against support for Columbus' scheme, and he had proved them wrong. At least he believed he had done so. The main objection to his trip was that the Indies and Japan were simply too far away, and that Columbus could never make it in any ship available at that time in history. In his final entry in his journal, which he presented to Queen Isabella, his principal champion, Columbus took a shot at his opponents. "Of this voyage I observe that the will of God hath miraculously been set forth (as may be seen from this journal) by the many signal miracles that He hath shown on the voyage and for myself, who for so great a time was in the court of Your Highness, *with the opposition and against the opinion of so many high personages of your household, who were all against me, alleging this undertaking to be folly,* which I hope in our Lord will be to the greater glory of Christianity, which to some extent has already occurred" (Morrison 61).

Thus, rather than being gracious, Columbus, to use a modern saying, "rubbed their noses in it," and created some lasting enemies. These enemies eventually led to doubts in him by the King and the Queen. This precipitated their sending Francisco de Bobadilla to conduct an investigation of Columbus' governorship. Columbus welcomed, even invited, the royal investigation, believing it would clear his name of various charges made against him. The queen chose Knight Commander Bobadilla. One principal charge was that Columbus was not being fair to the European settlers. Oddly, this would seem to contradict the persistent accusations in modern times that Columbus was oppressing the natives (De Seno). When Bobadilla approached the settlement, he was stunned to see two Spaniards hanging from newly-constructed gallows. The men had been executed for rebellion and "hideous deeds they had committed against the Indians." It was Columbus' intent that their deaths would serve two purposes, one as an example to the rest of the colonists, but also to demonstrate to the natives that the "rule of law applied to his own men" (Delaney 181). When Columbus arrived back at the settlement to welcome Bobadilla, the royal investigator immediately arrested the admiral, placing him chains! Bobadilla released the other rebel prisoners, and reversed Columbus' peace policy with the Indians. Bobadilla told the rebels to "(T)ake as many advantages as you can, since you don't know how long this will last" (Delaney 182).

The "investigation" consisted of arresting Columbus and his brothers for alleged mistreatment of the Indians, and sending them back to Spain. Not surprisingly, Bobadilla then appointed himself governor to replace Columbus. Spain's monarchs released Columbus as soon as he was returned to Spain, exonerating him (De Seno).

As Ardon has written, history shows that the charges against him were "absolutely false."

Bobadilla was recalled by Ferdinand and Isabella, and he drowned on the way back to Spain. Ironically, out of several ships, the one carrying Columbus' personal belongings survived the voyage across the Atlantic (De Seno).

Of course, it is all well and good to defend Columbus from these unfair libels that he was a murderer, a slave-trader, a rapist, and the like, but what did he actually accomplish? First of all, his modern critics choose to belittle his many achievements. "He did not discover America. The Indians did that. In fact, Columbus was not even the first European to make it to the western hemisphere," is typical of the statements they make.

Actually, he *did* discover America, in the sense that a person "discovers" a love of music, or some such. Despite the probability that other Europeans had made it to North America first, before Columbus the continents were unaware of the others, so in a very real sense, he is responsible for the European discovery of America. Vikings under the leadership of Leif Erickson almost certainly landed in North America, somewhere, almost 500 years later. Others probably preceded him. But none of these folks changed the course of history. Columbus did that. What Columbus accomplished was that he ended the disconnected histories of the world. No "Indian" did that, and certainly no Norwegian. As Morrison says, "We now honor Columbus for doing something that he had never intended to do . . . Yet we are right in so honoring him because no other sailor had the persistence, the knowledge, and the sheer guts to sail thousands of miles into the unknown ocean until he found land" (8-9).

Columbus first went to sea at age ten, and loved it. He grew into one of the greatest sea captains of his day, beyond all doubt. His first wife,

Dona Felipe Prestrello e Moniz, was the daughter of Bartholomew Pere-strello. Perestrello's father was a friend of the famous Prince Henry the Navigator of Portugal. Through this marriage, Columbus came into pos-session of some of the most accurate maps of the day. In someone else's hands, they were a curiosity, while in his hands, they changed the world. By age 32, he was a master mariner in the Portuguese merchant service (Morrison 15-16).

At this time, the Indies, by which was meant most of the eastern part of Asia, which included what is now India, Burma, China, Japan, and Indonesia, were alive in the imaginations of western Europeans. The Indies were believed to be lands of vast wealth, with desired goods such as silver and gold, silk, cotton, spices, and perfumes. Desire to trade for these precious goods led Prince Henry of Portugal to develop a naval school so as to develop an all-water trade route to the East. Eventually, the Por-tuguese would opt to do so by sailing around the southern tip of Africa, then on east to eastern Asia.

Columbus had a different idea.

He believed a better all-water route was by sailing west, to reach "the East." This rested upon the belief that the world was a sphere. This was cer-tainly not unique to Columbus. Washington Irving created the myth that Columbus was almost alone in believing that the world was round, and disbelief in the roundness of the earth caused him to be rejected by the Spanish so many times. Actually, educated people of the day all believed in the roundness of the earth. It certainly contradicted no Christian belief. Some even noted Isaiah 40:22, in the Bible, which indicated the round-ness of the earth.

The problem was that Columbus grossly underestimated the size of the earth, by about one-fourth. One reason for this is that Columbus had, like many others in Europe, read Marco Polo's accounts of his 13th century travels to China to the court of Kublai Khan. Polo had given wildly inac-curate estimates of the distance that had stretched the eastward distance to Japan. Had Polo's calculations been correct, Japan would be located approximately the same line of longitude as western Cuba, and Chat-tanooga, Tennessee! No wonder Columbus believed a trip to the Indies by sailing west was so logical (Morrison 18).

After Bartholomew Dias successfully rounded the southern tip of Africa in 1488, the Portuguese lost interest in Columbus' idea of a western all-water trade route. Columbus was unable to persuade the Spanish, either. The Talavera Commission, as it was called, appointed by the Spanish monarchs to consider Columbus' proposed western voyage, turned him down in 1490. They believed, correctly, that no ship of the day could make the 10,000-mile trip to Japan. But, Queen Isabella did offer that he could reapply once the Spanish Muslims (Moors) were finally driven out of Spain. (Morrison 25). The Moors were what was left of the Muslim invasion of the country in the 8th century.

So, Columbus waited. In the meantime, he seldom missed Mass, was known to refrain from uttering oaths or cursing, and held firm to belief in Jesus Christ as his Savior. He would need his faith to sustain him, because, as Morrison said, more disappointments awaited him (25).

After the fall of the Moorish kingdom of Granada in January, 1492, Columbus' hopes were dashed again. This time, Ferdinand gave what appeared to be the final no. Discouraged, Columbus traveled toward Seville. He was not giving up his dream. His intention was to go to France, and appeal to the French king, Charles VIII. At this point, one person changed the course of history. Luis de Sanange, the keeper of King Ferdinand's privy purse, urged Isabella to back Columbus, and she relented. A messenger overtook Columbus, and the rest, as they say, is history (Morrison 27).

Columbus was awarded the title of admiral, which meant he would have "admiralty jurisdiction" over the ocean and all new lands. He was promised 10% of all expected profits.

He gathered a crew of about 90 men, who joined together in saying the Lord's Prayer before leaving Spain. On the trip, when they mistakenly thought they had spotted land, the crew burst into singing, "Gloria in escelis Deo" (Morrison 38).

But, as the days dragged on, and they got further and further from home, the men began to grumble. There was concern they might not be able to make it home, not that they would fall of the end of the earth, or that they might be swallowed by a great sea monster.

Finally, on October 7th, a large flock of birds flew over the ship, and it was thought land was very close. But, by the 10th, there was still no land, and there was danger of mutiny. Many men called on Columbus to turn around. At that point, he reluctantly promised that if they did not spot land within three days, they would abandon their quest, and return to Spain.

Then, at 2 a.m., on Octobe 12th, the lookout shouted, "Tierra! Tierra!," which is to say, "Land, Land!" They landed off a small island in the Bahamas, which Columbus named San Salvador (Holy Savior).

But they were not alone.

They were met by some of the Taino branch of the Arawak language group. Apparently, they had come from the mainland in dugout canoes, and armed with only wooden spears, had wrested the Bahamas and most of Cuba from a more primitive tribe within the previous century (Morrison 43).

Columbus observed that it would be easy to "convert these people," indicating his principal desire was to convert them to Christianity (Morrison 43).

He was the first European to see Indian corn, and the first to see tobacco (used as cigars by the Taino). And, of course, thinking he had made it to the Indies, he referred to these indigenous peoples as "Indians." The name stuck for centuries, until in modern times, it has become more "politically correct" to describe these people as "native Americans," as though they called themselves that any more than they called themselves Indians.

Relations were so cordial at first that the Indians requested some Spaniards remain behind. Columbus had no trouble finding volunteers (they evidently believed they could find gold).

Columbus made four trips to the "New World," as it was soon to be called, but he never made it to Asia, nor did he ever make contact with the Grand Khan.

Myths surround Christopher Columbus. But, the biggest myth is that he did not accomplish anything, at least nothing positive. Certainly, Columbus was not a perfect man. As Morrison said, "He had his faults and his defects, but they were largely the defects of the qualities that made him great—-his indomitable will, his superb faith in God and his own mission as the Christ-bearer to the lands beyond the seas, his stubborn persistence despite neglect, poverty, and discouragement. But there was no flaw, no dark side for the most outstanding and essential of his qualities—-his seamanship" (Morrison 10).

Because of Columbus, millions of individual souls in the western hemisphere were exposed to the Christian religion. While this is, for some, at best a non-issue, and for others an outright negative, it carried both eternal and temporal positive consequences for the indigenous peoples of America. Human sacrifice and cannibalism soon came to an end. In Europe, life was improved dramatically by the introduction of new foods, such as okra, tomatoes, Indian corn (maize), squash, and more. Indeed, if one were to make a "short list" of the persons in history who had done the most to improve the lives of more human beings, a name that would have to be on that list would be that of Christopher Columbus.

LIBEL #9

MARIE ANTOINETTE IS RESPONSIBLE FOR THE FRENCH REVOLUTION

"I have ever believed that had there been no queen,
there would have been no revolution."

So declared Thomas Jefferson, who, like many Americans of his day looked with favor upon the French Revolution, especially in the period before it degenerated into the bloodbath known as the Reign of Terror. The "queen," of course, was Marie Antoinette, who is viewed in the popular culture as the prototype of the haughty, selfish, and callous royal who looked down upon the common people of her country as something less than human.

Most of what the average person believes about her is not true. Perhaps no quotation in history more falsely casts a person in a greater unfavorable light than her alleged response to the statement that the poor have no bread: "Then let them eat cake." This sums up how Marie Antoinette is remembered by most, but she never said any such thing, and in fact, the quotation stands almost directly opposite of her life as the wife of French King Louis XVI.

Today, she continues to be libeled, as she was in her own day, and this false portrait of her is often used to cast women of today in an unfavorable light. Nancy Reagan was often compared to Antoinette when the first lady expressed a desire to buy some new china for the White House during the deep recession of 1980-82. Michelle Obama has also been labeled another Antoinette as a result of her multiple taxpayer-funded vacations, despite the tough economic times of the past few years. Interestingly, in contrast, when Jackie Kennedy dressed lavishly, it was considered "style," but generally American first ladies must always be on guard against the "Marie Antoinette" label. It is also a convenient comparison for the wives of foreign leaders the American media does not like. All one has to do is remember Imelda Marcos and her many shoes.

Accusations against Antoinette are numerous, but Jefferson's comment that she was the principal cause of the French Revolution is, outside of the quotation falsely attributed to her ("Then let them eat cake!"), the one charge into which all the other indictments can be bundled. To better understand this false charge, one must look at European history in the years leading up to the Revolution. Another "revolution" led to the marriage of the 14 year old Marie Antoinette to the future king (dauphin) of France. For many years, the two most powerful dynasties of Europe, the Hapsburgs and the Bourbons, had struggled for domination of the European continent. The center of the Hapsburg Dynasty was Austria, while the home of the Bourbon Dynasty was France, although both had relatives in key positions in other nations. Then, in 1756, after years of contests and wars, the two nations achieved what was then known as the "Diplomatic Revolution," in which the two nations settled their difference. As was typical of the day, the pretty young Austrian princess, Marie Antoinette, was used as a pawn of international politics to seal the alliance with a marriage to the boy who would someday be King Louis XVI.

On the surface, it appeared that the marriage would cement the alliance, leading to years of peace for a war-weary continent. At first, Antoinette was quite popular in France, but the situation into which the girl had been placed was actually very toxic. One person who considered the breaking of the French-Austrian alliance as the great ambition of his life was Prussia's Frederick the Great. The Hohenzollern family of Prussia desired the dominant position in the Holy Roman Empire (now basically the nation of Germany) then ruled by the Hapsburgs, and the alliance with France, consummated by the marriage of Marie Antoinette to France's next king threatened this ambition. For her part, Antoinette disliked the Prussians. In *The French Revolution: A Study in Democracy*, Nesta Webster wrote, "Marie Antoinette paid heavily for her aversion to Prussia. There can be no doubt whatever that certain of the libels and seditious pamphlets published against her before and during the Revolution were circulated by [Prussian envoy to France] von der Goltz at the instigation of the king of Prussia" (Webster 27).

She was also a victim of decades of anti-Austrian feeling among both the nobles and the common people of France. While the populace no doubt felt relief that the alliance and the marriage reduced the chances of yet another war, it is perhaps too much to expect that the long period of animosity toward all things Austrian could so easily be eliminated.

The marriage also threatened the dynastic ambitions of the Bourbon's chief rivals for the French throne, the Orleans family. Cousins of the Bourbons, the Orleans family were next in line should the Bourbon family fail to produce heirs. The Duke of Orleans in particular believed himself more capable than the Bourbon heir to the throne. He was also jealous of his cousin's marriage to the pretty Austrian princess (Webster 24).

Another dark factor, which became increasingly important as the Revolutions itself drew nearer, was the presence of a large number of subversive "secret societies," such as the Jacobin Clubs, which drank freely from the most radical ideas of the Enlightenment. Many of these radicals desired the uprooting of the Old Regime, and over time, the foreign-born queen of France became a convenient target in their assaults upon the institution of the monarchy.

It is clear that each of these three sources of animosity toward Antoinette all had their own separate agendas, but the road to implementation of each diverse goal all went through her. As a result of years of scurrilous attacks, she was finally transformed into the wicked villain of popular imagination.

In the years leading up to the French Revolution, pamphlets circulated widely in France, especially in Paris, creating a Marie Antoinette of unbelievable monstrosity, one not even credible for a comic book villain. Yet, it was widely believed at the time. Chantal Thomas, in the book, *The Wicked Queen: The Origins of the Myth of Marie-Antoinette*, was taken aback by the intensity of the hatred directed at her. "I became more and more amazed and fascinated by the awesome monstrosity of Marie-Antoinette portrayed in the pamphlets, by her flagrant unreality" (Thomas 10).

The pamphlets portrayed a woman "whose capacity for evil exceeded, by a long shot, all bounds of plausibility," as she was, over the course of many years, condemned as an adulterous, traitor, sodomite, lesbian, incestuous mother, infant murderer, and all sorts of vile crimes. As Thomas said, it is "astonishing" that such tales could ever seem plausible, and yet, "the myth still hovers over the cadaver." Mme de Stael, the daughter of Louis XVI's ex-controller general, Jacques Necker, wrote at the time, "(N)o queen . . . has ever seen herself libeled so publicly" (11, 20, 21, 25).

All manner of evil was blamed on her. One pamphlet even went so far as to say, "(A)ll our calamities, past, present, and to come, have always been and will always be her doing." She was compared to the evil queen of the Bible, Jezebel. Even her desire to go with some friends out to see the sun rise one morning led to a pamphlet, implying something evil must have been involved. She was accused in the pamphlets of having an incestuous relationship with her own brother, the king's brother, and her own son, as well as sexual encounters with women and even animals (59, 71, 100, 110).

One book was published in 1792, with the amazing title, *The List of all the People with whom the Queen Has Had Depraved Relations*. A song in one pamphlet included the line, "She spends her life screwing anything that moves." Although she drank little to no alcohol, she was accused of habitual drunkenness and drunken orgies (108, 122, 194).

If her alleged sexual affairs was not enough evil, she was even accused of poisoning her own son, and trying to do the same to her husband, the king (133).

But she considered the accusations so absurd that no one actually could believe them. While her mother, Queen Maria Theresa of Austria, expressed concern as early as 1774 (and the libels would only get much worse), about the negative effects of the pamphlets, Marie Antoinette wrote her mother in November, 1775: "(T)he songs are so flat and in such bad taste that they are successful neither with the public or high society" (51).

She was wrong, underestimating the capacity for gullibility, especially when a lie is repeated for long enough, without any contrary expression of the facts. We see the same methods used today to destroy the reputations of innocent people.

Count Fersen, a friend of both the king and the queen, said that by the time of the Revolution, there were as many as a dozen pamphlets produced *each day*, and expressed amazement that the "printing offices suffice for them all" (Quill 206).

Where did the money originate for all these pamphlets? It appears that the two main sources of financing were from the Prussian government, which had the motive of splitting the French-Austrian alliance; and the king's distant cousin, Phillipe d' Orleans, who was known to employee pamphleteers to keep up an incessant attack on the royal couple. The Duke of Orleans was even wealthier than the king himself, and he was willing to spend some of his wealth to accomplish his desire to replace Louis XVI as king of France (Thomas 46; Webster 27).

While characterized at the time (and today) as uncaring and callous to the sufferings of the poor of France, the real Marie Antoinette was much different. Examples abound. Her early years in France were marred by difficulties between her and her teen-aged husband, the heir to the throne. She wanted to be a good wife for the young Louis, who loved to go hunting, so she often went with him. During one hunt at Fontainebleau, a stag gored a peasant wine-grower, causing the man's wife to pass out. Antoinette jumped out of her carriage, and went to the woman, giving her a whiff of perfume and comforted her, even offering money. She conveyed the man in her own carriage (Thomas 84).

She lodged and fed 12 poor families, at her own expense, at Trianon. She founded the Society of Ladies of Maternal Charity. Another time she stopped her carriage for over an hour to aid an injured person, and waited until a surgeon was located (Thomas 84).

Writing in *Marie Antoinette: The Journey*, historian Antonia Fraser directly challenged the myth that the French queen ever said, "Let them eat cake."

"As a handy journalistic cliché, it may never die," Fraser wrote, adding that "such ignorant behavior would have been quite out of character. The unfashionably philanthropic Marie Antoinette would have been far more likely to bestow her own cake impulsively upon the starving people before her" (Fraser xx).

Before the flood of ubiquitous pamphlets poisoned the opinions of the populace of Paris, she was quite popular. One time, when she and Louis had ascended to the throne, their walk through the Tuileries Palace gardens, there was such a large and enthusiastic crowd that they were unable to move for almost an hour. In the late spring of 1773, she wrote,

"How fortunate we are, given our rank, to have gained the love of a whole people" (Fraser 104).

The accusations of sexual depravity are also false. Contrary to the picture painted by the pamphlets, she was actually disgusted at the sexual immorality she witnessed at the French court. Her husband's grandfather, King Louis XV, was well-known for his adulterous lifestyle, causing Antoinette to describe the king's mistress Du Barry as "the most stupid and impertinent creature" (Fraser 87).

She rejected more than one sexual advance while queen. Madam Compan ridiculed her personal modesty as "extreme." Her brother told King Leopold, "Her virtue is intact, even strict." It is thought that one of the reasons that the Duke of Orleans hated her so much was that she had turned away his advances so strongly. Unlike his grandfather, Louis XV, and his more distant ancestor, Louis XIV, Louis XVI refused to take a mistress, clearly adoring his "delightful" wife from Austria. "Everyone would like me to take a mistress, but I have no intention of doing so," he said (Fraser, 144; Quill, 142).

He adored Marie, at least eventually. Apparently the marriage of the 15 year old Louis and 14 year old Marie was not consummated for seven years. Finally, her brother, Emperor Joseph, came to France in 1777 and lectured them separately on the facts of life. Different authors have come to diverse conclusions as to why the young couple waited so long to begin producing children, but once they did, it appears the two had as happy a marriage as could be expected in a royal marriage of the day (Fraser 156).

Most of the accusations of a sexual nature against her are beyond the realm of reality. Some authors speculate that she did have one indiscretion, with a foreign nobleman, Count Fersen. Others, however, dismiss this accusation, as well, arguing that logistics and discretion make any such affair "unlikely." Fersen clearly had affection for both the king and the queen. Shortly before Fersen left to go to America to assist the colonies in their war to secede from the British Empire, the Duchesse de Saint-James told him that she had heard rumors of his "conquest" of the queen. "Are you abandoning your conquest?" she asked him. Fersen replied, "If I had made one, I would not abandon it" (Fraser 181).

This is not to say the Austrian-born French queen was perfect. She was not. In the early years of her time in France, she spent her allowance almost as fast as she received it, usually on clothes and gambling, but also on charity. Her spending is often cited as the principal cause of the French Revolution, which is absurd. But this myth is still believed today, and was a widely-held view in her day, winning her the nickname, "Madame Deficit," as France sunk deeper into debt and into bankruptcy (Fraser 141; Quill 164).

It was *not* her spending that was the main problem, however. *All* court expenditure was only six to seven percent in 1788, while almost half of the annual spending was going just to service the national debt. (Fraser 255). How had France run up such an enormous debt?

Most of the debt was incurred before Louis XVI came to the throne, from the four wars of Louis XIV, followed by the Seven Years' War (known as the French and Indian War in America) under Louis XV. The mounting debt was seen as such a problem that it is said that Louis XV expressed concern that following him would come "the deluge." Some say it was Louis XIV who said it. The point is, even if no one said it, it was an accurate prophecy.

The principal source of financial difficulties for France was that the nation had fought so many wars over such a long period of time. The fact is that Louis XVI inherited a mess. But, he made it worse by choosing to involve France in the conflict between Great Britain and their North American colonists. While Americans even use the French intervention as a justification for American intervention in the affairs of other countries today, it could be cited as a reason to refrain from foreign adventures. It is not certain if Louis XVI could have avoided national bankruptcy even if he had opted to stay out of the American Revolution, but he no doubt deepened the problem and hastened his own demise by jumping in.

Antoinette played no role in this decision. She was more concerned with her own family than international politics. Louis was reluctant to intervene in the American Revolution, and his financial advisor, Anne-Robert-Jacque Turgot was adamantly opposed. While Turgot was sympathetic to the American cause, he argued that France's financial difficulty was so grave, that the nation simply lacked the funds to support the American colonists. His guiding principles he conveyed to Louis were, "No bankruptcy, no increase of taxation, no borrowing." He was able to reduce the national debt, and worked for a free trade in grain. In this, Turgot encountered the stiff opposition of many powerful French nobles, such as the Duke of Orleans, who benefitted financially from the domestic grain trade. Had Louis continued to follow Turgot's frugal policies, perhaps the French Revolution could have been averted. But he sought advice elsewhere, and dismissed Turgot. While Antoinette did not particularly care for Turgot, for other reasons, she had no role in his dismissal (Fraser 150-151).

Finally, Louis gave into the desire of his chief minister, Charles Gravier, comte de Vergennes, to go to war against the British. The apparent motive was simply revenge for France's crushing defeat in the Seven Years' War. Louis later expressed regret that Vergennes had talked him into this military adventure. Not only would the war bring on the financial crisis of the late 1780s, revolutionary doctrines grown in the soil of Britain's American colonies were brought home to France in 1789. Mixed with the more radical Enlightenment ideas in France, the libelous pamphlets, and the plotting of the Duke of Orleans and other nobles, it created the poisoned environment that cost the royal couple first their thrones, and finally their heads.

An event that further sullied the queen's reputation, despite her complete innocence in the whole sordid incident, was the "Diamond Necklace Affair." This complicated episode illustrates how her enemies were either ignorant of the facts, or were simply malicious liars.

During her earlier years in France, she enjoyed the purchase of diamonds, but this interest had waned considerably with the births of her children, and perhaps her own higher maturity level. Perhaps she finally got all the diamonds she wanted. Charles August Boehmer was an international jeweler, who ran a shop in Paris with a partner, Paul Bassenge, who had previous dealings with the queen. But, he was unable to interest her in a very expensive diamond necklace originally intended for Madame du Barry, the mistress of Louis XV. She rejected the 647-diamond necklace repeatedly, saying that her jewel cases were "rich enough," adding that France had more need of ships than diamonds.

Madame Lamotte, an impoverished descendant of past Valois nobility, hatched an idea to gain a position at court, while Prince de Rohan, the Cardinal of France, had a continuing desire to regain his position in the queen's inner circle. Combined with Boehmer's need to recoup his expenditure on the expensive diamond, this led to the nefarious scheme known as the "Diamond Necklace Affair."

Lamotte convinced the two men that she was the lesbian lover of Marie Antoinette (thus showing the insidious effects of years of libelous pamphlets against the queen), and that the queen really did desire the diamond, but was just in financial difficulty. Seeing his opportunity to ingratiate himself with the queen, Cardinal Rohan obtained the necklace from Boehmer and gave it to Lamotte.

Lamotte had met Rohan in 1783, and learned of Rohan's desire to obtain the queen's favor. The plot depended upon convincing Rohan that the queen not only wanted the necklace, but would make installments payments for it. A professional actress and prostitute, Nical d' Olivia, who bore a resemblance to Antoinette, impersonated her in the semi-dark promenade of Palais-Royal near the Temple of Love, where the Marie Antoinette imposter expressed a desire for the necklace. After the necklace was obtained from Boehmer, Lamotte's husband, Comte de Lamotte, took it to London to sell, explaining to prospective buyers that he had inherited the diamonds from his mother.

After Rohan advanced the money, duped into believing the queen desired the necklace, he soon wondered why she had not yet worn it. Boehmer thought he had sold the queen the necklace for one and one-half million francs, but both Rohan and Boehmer had been scammed.

Boehmer was mystified as to why Antoinette had not begun payments on the diamond, so he wrote her what he considered a diplomatic request for payment. "Madame," the letter began. "We are at the summit of happiness to dare to think the latest arrangements which have been proposed to us and to which we have submitted with zeal and respect, are a new proof of our own submission and devotion to the orders of your Majesty. We have real satisfaction in the thought that the most beautiful set of diamonds in the world will be at the service of the greatest and best of queens."

Antoinette was somewhat baffled by the letter, but concluded that it was simply a new solicitation to buy a diamond necklace that she had already rejected, multiple times.

Finally, Rohan confronted Antoinette about the affair at the Feast of the Assumption of the Virgin Mary, on August 15, 1785. The king asked Rohan who had commissioned him to conduct this necklace transaction, and Rohan responded that it was Comtesse de Lamotte Valois. Rohan then showed them the letter that Comtesse had supposedly received from the queen. When the king read the letter, he quickly knew that it was not his wife's handwriting, and became enraged, believing his queen's good name had been "compromised."

Rohan was arrested and sent to the Bastille to await trial. The ensuing trials were a disaster to Antoinette's reputation. Rohan asked for a trial before the Parlement of Paris, where he was acquitted by the nobility on a charge of insulting the queen. The Duke of Orleans was among those in opposition to Rohan's conviction, siding with the queen's enemies. Rohan did have to apologize, seek the king's pardon, give up all offices, make a donation to the poor, and be forever banished from the court.

At Lamotte's trial, her defense was that Antoinette was in the midst of an adulterous affair with Rohan! Lamotte was convicted, but escaped from prison, later concocting a tale that *she* was the queen's lover. In the end, the whole sordid affair was spun by the pamphlets that the queen had stiffed a jeweler, and had involved herself in sexual affairs with both Rohan and Lamotte (for more details on the Diamond Necklace Affair, see http://www.marie-antoinette.org; Fraser 226-243; Thomas 48).

By the time of the Diamond Necklace Affair, the fiscal affairs of the nation were reaching a crisis, and the belief that Antoinette was more interested in diamonds than in the nation's financial health contributed greatly to the "perfect storm" about to overwhelm both the king and the queen. One hundred and seventy-three posts were eliminated from the queen's household alone, but the nobles who were also needed, and expected, to join in the fiscal retrenchment greatly resented any infringement upon their privileges. Desperate, Louis XVI favored many fiscal reforms, including taxes upon the nobles, and a drastic reduction in spending.

The Parlement of Paris, controlled by the French nobles, refused to endorse *any* fiscal reform which adversely affected them. Under the legal structure used in France at the time, new laws had to be registered by the Parlement, and guided by the opposition of the king's cousin, Phillipe (the Duke of Orleans), they refused to do so. Louis was taken aback by their vitriolic quarreling. Finally, in exasperation, after seven hours of their inaction, the king issued an edict on November 19, 1787, ordering the registration of the reforms. The Duke of Orleans yelled a protest that Louis XVI's action was illegal. Louis retorted that the action *was* legal, "because I wish it." He later ordered the banishment of his rebellious cousin (Quill 193-194).

According to Carolly Erickson Quill, in *To the Scaffold: the Life of Marie Antoinette*, the Duke of Orleans had always resented the king, and used every opportunity to oppose his royal cousin, casting himself as the people's champion, and an opponent of "oppressive government." Madame La Tour du Pin said that the Duke "corrupted everything within his reach." He was notorious for his drinking parties, where he often stripped naked with several females, and would jump into the water. As Quill put it: "(I)n the turmoil of the late 1780s, he saw his chance to seize power, and was determined to make the most of it" (190-192).

In an effort to weaken the opposition of the powerful nobles and strengthen the bourgeoisie, Louis moved to call a meeting of the Estates-General. The Estates-General had not been called in well over a hundred years, but he hoped that this could break the logjam posed by the Parlement of Paris, which continued to block a reform of the tax system of France. The Estates-General was divided into three estates, the first being the clergy (which meant the higher-ranking church officers, like bishops), the second estate being the nobility, leaving the rest of the nation in the so-called Third Estate. In reality, the bourgeoisie (mostly the middle class merchants) would control the Third Estate. Louis expected this group to support him against the recalcitrant nobles, led by his ambitious cousin, the Duke of Orleans (Quill 190-192).

A British visitor, Arthur Young, remarked at a dinner party in October, 1787, that the prevailing opinion was that France was on the verge of revolution, largely because of the "enormous deficit." The king, Young said, was "well-intentioned, but lacking in sufficient mental resources to govern decisively" (Quill 192).

The "perfect storm" was gathering. The ideas of "liberty" had been brought back from America by French soldiers. That intervention was, by far, the major cause of the impending bankruptcy of the country. By 1788, the treasury was empty, and the financiers refused to make any more loans. The desperate government resorted to issuing promissory notes, bearing 5% interest. The king's minister, Jacques Necker, who had been ousted, was recalled at the urging of the queen. Somehow, Necker obtained new credit, perhaps with the hope that the meeting of the Estates-General in seven months could lead to a solution of the crisis (Quill 199-201).

The "perfect storm" included a somewhat literal element, as severe hail-storms did great damage to the potential harvest around Paris. The winter of 1788-89 was particularly severe. With the severe shortage, bread prices increased dramatically. Stories were spread in Paris that the Duke of Orleans had sold paintings, so as to donate eight million francs to feed the hungry, but the charitable efforts of the queen went largely unnoticed (Quill 204).

The king solicited the suggestions of the people of France in what were called the *cahiers*, or list of concerns from the provinces for the Estates-General to consider. None of the cahiers even hinted that the king should step down, and none expressed any criticism of Marie Antoinette, but almost all the cahiers assumed the nation was heading to a limited, constitutional monarchy, with an expansion of the people's liberties. Some expressed more immediate and practical concerns, such as one from Menouville, a village in the Paris basin, which pleaded, "We beg His Majesty to have pity on our farmland because of the hail we have had" (Quill 206-209). Exactly what the king was supposed to do about hail, or its effects upon the land, was not mentioned.

Finally, in May, 1789, amidst great pomp and ceremony, the Estates-General opened for the first time since the days of Louis XIII. In the opening procession of the Estates-General, from Notre Dame to the cathedral of Saint Louis, with the king walking at the end, there were shouts of, "Long live King Orleans!" As the carriage carrying the queen rolled by, there were shouts of, "The Duke of Orleans forever!" (Quill 208-209).

Instead of serious financial discussions, the Estates-General broke into procedural disputes, over whether the three estates should vote separately (as they had always done so before), or whether they would vote together as one body. Louis had doubled the membership of the Third Estate, causing some within that group to take the opportunity to advance the position of the bourgeoisie. While the Estates-General wrangled, the king and queen were distracted by their dying son, who passed in June. The grieving royal couple left for a week in seclusion, leaving behind the various factions to jockey for power. Bread shortages intensified, and the Paris Mob rioted (Quill 215-217).

On June 10th, the Third Estate urged the nobles and the clergy to unite with them. Many did, and on June 17th, they proclaimed themselves the National Assembly of France. On June 20th, the new National Assembly found the meeting hall closed, so the deputies went to a nearby indoor tennis court to escape rain. There, they took the Tennis-Court Oath, in which they pledged to not adjourn until they had a adopted a new constitution for France. Louis brought troops closer to the capital, for protection, and ordered all deputies to join the National Assembly on June 27th (Quill 218-219).

As the grain shortage grew even more severe, the Duke of Orleans began bribing hungry Parisians to rebel and overthrow the government. Thousands stood outside bakeries all day, waiting for bread. Rumors of all sorts both alarmed and enraged the populace. One rumor had it that the king had even mined the meeting hall of the National Assembly (Quill 220).

Then, on July 13th, bourgeoisie electors of Paris created a governing committee for the city, and mobs began to break into gunsmith's shops, searching for weapons. A new rumor on July 14th caused the greatest alarm yet. Soldiers were supposedly poised to attack the city! This led the mob to attack the Hotel des Invalides, where they found nearly 30,000 muskets. But, since there were few cartridges, and only small stores of powder, the mob was pointed to the Bastille. The mob was told the prison fortress contained vast stores of both cartridges and gun powder (Quill 221-222).

The Bastille was a 14th century castle that Louis XVI would have already destroyed, but he lacked the funds. At one time, especially during the absolute rule of the "Sun King," Louis XIV, the prison had housed hundreds of political prisoners. Now, it had only seven prisoners, four of which were forgers, one person in the jail for incest, and two others, who were probably insane.

But, all of this was not known to the mob. They believed it still held hundreds of political dissidents within its thick walls. The mob demanded entrance to the Bastille. The governor of the Bastille, De Launay, chose to capitulate without a fight. The mob then proceeded to butcher him, stabbing him repeatedly, in addition to shooting him. A sword was used, along with a pocket knife, to decapitate him. His severed head was then placed at the end of a pike.

Rumors spread that hundreds of political prisoners had been liberated from the Bastille.

Antoinette had seen enough, and urged her husband to take the opportunity for them to escape the country. Louis urged calm, that they should stay. His wife proved to be the better prophet. Rumor followed rumor, mostly untrue, leading to more and more violence. Then, the story made its way across the city, and eventually across the nation, around the world, and into the popular legend of Marie Antoinette. When told the people have no bread to eat, the story went, the queen had haughtily replied, "Then let them eat cake." Of course it was not true, but so many lies about her had been repeated over the past several years, that most of the population evidently believed it was true, as absurd as the story was (Quill 236).

It is doubtful that anything besides immediate flight could have saved Louis XVI and Marie Antoinette at this point. But, Louis hesitated, ignoring his wife's pleadings. On October 5, 1789, agents of the Duke of Orleans entered several Paris cafes, calling for the king and queen to be forcibly moved from their nearby palace at Versailles into Paris. Hundeds of women, and men dressed as women, responded, gathered at the Hotel de Ville, and made the relatively short walk to Versailles, bringing the king and queen back to Paris as virtual prisoners (Quill 228, 236, 238).

Once the king and queen were relocated, by force, in the old Tuileries palace in Paris, their fate was most likely sealed. When the National Assembly made the unfortunate decision to also leave Versailles, and follow the royal couple into Paris, the nation's fate was probably sealed, as well. Now, the entire government of France was at the mercy of the violent Paris Mob. And those who led the Mob, doing their thinking for them.

The revolution became increasingly radical, and violent. Louis XVI was eventually sentenced to death by the National Convention, called to write a new constitution for France. His own cousin, the Duke of Orleans (now calling himself Phillipe Egalite, hoping to ingratiate himself with the revolutionary spirit of the day), had gained a seat in the National Convention, and voted for the king's death. Perhaps the Duke should have been made aware of the old Chinese proverb, "He who foolishly seeks power by riding the back of a tiger, often ends up inside." As the Reign of Terror intensified, Phillipe Egalite was among thousands who followed his royal cousin to the guillotine.

Not content with the king's death, the revolutionaries were soon clamoring for the queen's blood, as well. Now dismissed as the Widow Capet, Marie Antoinette faced "trial" before the Revolutionary Tribunal. The verdict was a foregone conclusion, which was guilty, followed by death. She was accused of treason, because she did not believe in the principles of the Revolution. (Of course, thousands of others also faced beheading for the same thing). Had every person who also despised the Revolution faced the guillotine, the death toll would have been in the millions, not just thousands.

Marie Antoinette was mostly silent in the face of her accusers, until they accused her of incest with her own son! She made an eloquent appeal to the mothers in the room, and seemed to win their sympathy, when she denounced that vile charge.

"I appeal to the conscience and feeling of every mother present, to declare if there be one amongst you who does not shudder at the idea of such horrors." But, it really did not matter. They were determined to murder her.

On October 16, 1794, Marie Antoinette, the woman thought guilty of multitudes of the most hideous of crimes and abominations, was paraded through the streets in a cart, and subjected to the jeering of the crowds. Her once long blonde hair had turned white, and her beauty had faded after months of captivity. Less than 40 years old, probably dying of tuberculosis, she now had the appearance of an old woman many years older.

Following her execution, the radicals leading the Reign of Terror caused thousands of others to follow her to the guillotine. Then the leaders of the Terror turned on each other, and France endured several more years of food shortages, violence, and war.

Today, those days are generally held as dark days, days of horror. While few hold the instigators of the Reign of Terror up as heroes, the image of Marie Antoinette has remain fixed in the popular mind. It is an image of a woman who was callous and heartless, and evil beyond description. A woman who dismissed the plea for those starving with the infamous retort, "Then let them eat cake."

It goes without saying that Marie Antoinette was no perfect woman. But to blame her for all the misery that led France into one of history's most terrible episodes—-the Reign of Terror—-is simply libel.

Sadly, the template of Marie Antoinette is dusted off from time to time, and used to attack other women in public life as "another Marie Antoinette."

But, if there was no first Marie Antoinette, at least not the comic book villain created by the pamphlets in the streets of late-18th century Paris, and perpetuated in the popular culture, then there can be no modern "Marie Antoinette."

LIBEL #10

HITLER WAS A CHAMPION OF CHRISTIANITY

Here we examine the flip-side of the "libel" that George Washington was a non-believer in Jesus Christ. There exists a significant overlap of those who smugly pronounce the majority of the Founding Fathers, such as Washington, as skeptics, infidels, and deists, while simultaneously proclaiming some of history's greatest monsters, such as Adolf Hitler, as "good Christians."

While Hitler is the favorite example of Christianity's enemies of a "good Christian," others who have committed mass murder usually make the short list of "model" Christians, at least for this group of militant atheists. Of course, any person who blows up an abortion clinic is penciled in on the list, along with preachers who have affairs, and the Westboro cultists. Klansmen are usually chalked up as "good Christians," as was Timothy McVeigh, executed for blowing up the Oklahoma City Murrah federal building. McVeigh was a self-described agnostic, but such inconvenient facts make little difference in these incessant efforts to sully the Christian faith.

But no one beats out Hitler.

Despite overwhelming evidence that Adolf Hitler actually despised Christianity, regardless of whether it is Catholic or Protestant, this libel that Hitler was some sort of champion of the Christian faith, is a persistent myth. The truth is the Hitler and his National Socialists (Nazis), as Alan Bullock wrote in his book, *Hitler: A Study in Tyranny*, "(O)nce the war was over, [Hitler] promised himself, he would root out and destroy the influence of the Christian churches" (219). In the short-run, Hitler the politician had to tread carefully, and not offend the German people, who were still mostly Christian. In fact, less than two percent of Germans identified themselves as atheists in 1939.

Hitler's relationship with Christianity, Laurence Rees contends, "was opportunistic." Writing in *The Dark Charisma of Adolf Hitler*, he concluded, "There is no evidence that Hitler himself, in his personal life, ever expressed any individual belief in the basic tenets of the Christian Church." While Hitler, as an ambitious politician, before the National Socialists came to power, could make such comments as, "Our movement is Christian," the truth is that Hitler had rejected any real belief in the basic beliefs of Christianity as a youth, growing up in Austria (17).

August Kubizek was Hitler's childhood friend in Linz, Austria. In his book, *The Young Hitler I Knew*, Kubizek makes it very clear that even in his teenage years, Hitler did not believe in Jesus Christ as anything more than a man. "For the entire time period that I knew Adolf Hitler," Kubizek recalled, "I do not think he ever attended mass. He knew that I went every Sunday with my parents." Although Hitler did not make any direct effort to restrain Kubizek to drop church attendance, he did tell his friend that he could not "understand" why he bothered.

"(O)ne day he came to me in great excitement and showed me a book about the Church witch-hunts, on another occasion one about the Inquisition," Kubizek wrote. The young Hitler added expressions of disgust. Hitler's widowed mother "always went to mass," Kubizek remembered, but Hitler, ignoring her begging that he do so, "never accompanied her" (95).

Kubizek met the young Hitler when the future German dictator was about 16. The year before, Hitler had undergone confirmation in the Catholic Church. Historian John Toland, in his book, *Adolf Hitler*, wrote about the 1904 ceremony, which took place in the cathedral in Linz. Hitler's confirmation sponsor said he almost had to "drag the words out him." The sponsor recalled that it was as if the "whole confirmation was repugnant to him" (22).

But, "Hitler's evident ability to simulate . . . an image of a leader keen to uphold and protect Christianity," was critical to his public image after he entered politics in the aftermath of the First World War, according to Ian Kershaw, in *The Hitler Myth: Image and Reality in the Third Reich*. Hitler was clever enough of a politician, who used religious rhetoric at times, and even quoted Scripture in public speeches, that as late as 1936 Cardinal Fauhlhaber thought Hitler believed in God, and the chancellor recognized Christianity as "the builder of western culture" (106, 109).

One reason that many Christian pastors and leaders were slow to realize that Hitler was a mortal foe of Christianity was not just his public rhetoric, but also that he was perceived as a superior alternative to the menace of atheistic communism. In the desperate times following the First World War, communists had come perilously close to seizing control of the German nation. Then, after the coming of the Great Depression, the openly atheistic communists were seen as a realistic threat to establish a Stalinist-style dictatorship upon the Germans.

At first, the National Socialists did not make a frontal assault upon the Christian religion, which had been dominant in Germany since the early years of the Middle Ages. Instead, Hitler and his henchmen pushed a "German" form of Christianity stripped of its "Jewish elements," or "Roman" features. While retaining the name of Christianity, it was to be a pagan form of the faith, emphasizing the German mythical gods of pre-Christian times, such as Wodin and Thor. In Hitler's "German," or "Positive Christianity," Jesus was transformed into a staunch Aryan, brandishing a sword, rather than wearing a crown of thorns (Fischer 358).

Martin Borman, a leading Nazi, said, "National Socialism and Christianity are irreconcilable." Borman continually pressed Hitler to launch an open assault upon the churches. While Hitler agreed with Borman's hostility to Christianity, he was going to bide his time. But, he told Borman that he, too, looked to the day when "only complete idiots stand in the pulpit and preach to old women" (Fischer 359).

As the National Socialist dictatorship grew stronger, the government pushed the "de-Christianizing of rituals related to birth, marriage, and death," according to Klaus Fischer in *Nazi Germany: A New History*. In 1938, carols and nativity plays were forbidden in the schools. Even the word "Christmas," celebrated in Germany for over a thousand years, was replaced by the secular "Yuletide" (360).

On November 13, 1933, a large "German Christian" rally was held in Berlin. Dr. Reinhardt Krause, a leader of the movement, publicly proposed an abandonment of the Old Testament, "with its tales of cattle merchants and pimps," and an extensive revision of the New Testament. Krause said that the teachings of Jesus needed to correspond "entirely with the demands of National Socialism." The government soon insisted that all of the churches exclude converts from Judaism (Shirer 237).

Among those murdered by the Nazis in a June 30, 1934 purge was Erich Klausener, leader of Catholic Action. Scores of Catholic publications were suppressed, and the privilege of the confessional booth was ignored. In regards to the Protestant opponents of the regime, Hitler told his aides, "They are insignificant little people" (Shirer 235).

In response to Hitler's "Positive" or "German" Christianity, a "Confessing Church" rose up in opposition. Only about three and one-half million Germans aligned with Hitler's church, with only 3,000 pastors, as compared to 17,000 "confessing" pastors. In May, 1934, the General Synod of the Confessing Church declared itself the legitimate Protestant Church in Germany, in opposition to the Nazi-backed "church." In May, 1936, they issued a memorandum to Hitler protesting the "anti-Christian tendencies of the regime." This was met by the arrest of hundreds of confessing pastors, with one signer of the memorandum, Dr. Weissler, murdered in a concentration camp, and the funds of the confessing church confiscated (Shirer 238).

It was clear where the National Socialists were headed—-a Germany devoid of historic Christianity. As quoted in William Shirer's *Rise and Fall of the Third Reich*, Nazi official Dr. Hans Kerrl ridiculed orthodox Christianity in February, 1937: "National Socialism is the doing of God's will . . . Dr. Zoellner and Count Galen [the Catholic bishop of Muenster] have tried to make clear to me that Christianity consists of faith in Christ as the Son of God. This makes me laugh . . . No, Christianity is not dependent upon the Apostle's Creed . . . True Christianity is represented by the party, and German people are called by the party and especially by the Fuehrer to a real Christianity" (239).

When the Confessing Church officially rejected an important element of what the National Socialists considered "real" Christianity, the whole racial aspect of the Nazi regime, about 700 ministers were arrested in 1935 (Fischer 361). Pastor Niemoeller, the principal leader of the Confessing Church, preached his last sermon in June, 1937. He told his congregation, quoting Scripture, "(W)e must obey God rather than man" (Shirer 239). Nazi police regularly spied on the sermons of Confessing

Church pastors (Kershaw 113). A few days later, Niemoeller, on July 1, 1937, was arrested and sentenced to prison for "abuse of the pulpit." He spent seven years in either prisons or concentration camps, until Dachau was liberated by Allied troops (Shirer 239).

Recalling his own tardiness in recognizing the sheer evil of the Nazi regime, and in opposing Hitler's anti-Christian actions, Niemoeller famously said, "First the Nazis went after the Jews, but I was not a Jew, so I did not object. Then they went after the Catholics, but I was not a Catholic, so I did not object. Then they went after the trade-unionists, but I was not a trade-unionist, so I did not object. Then they came after me, and there was no one else left to object" (Shirer 364).

Hundreds of nuns and priests were sent to concentration camps, as well, often on trumped-up charges of sexual immorality. More than one-third of the Catholic lower secular clergy were subjected to some form of political retribution (Shirer 363).

Albert Speer, Hitler's minister of armaments, published his memoirs several years after the war. In his *Inside the Third Reich*, Speer is certain that Hitler was only postponing the abolition of Christianity until a more "favorable" time, considering the traditional Christian faith an "absurdity," dismissing it as "humbug" all founded on "lies" (123). In *Hitler's Table Talk*, Hitler revealed that he believed Christianity was based on nothing but "myths." He predicted, "The dogma of Christianity gets worn away before the advances of science . . . Gradually the myths will crumble" (Trevor-Roper 59; 342-343).

According to Speer, Hitler considered Christianity too meek of a religion for the German nation. "You see it's been our misfortune to have the wrong religion. Why didn't we have the religion of the Japanese, who regard sacrifice to the Fatherland as the highest good? The Mohammeden religion too would have been more compatible to us than Christianity. Why did it have to be Christianity?" (123).

Shirer explained what Hitler planned to do about what he considered the misfortune of Christianity. "(T)he Nazi regime intended eventually to destroy Christianity in Germany, if it could, and substitute the old paganism of the early tribal Germanic gods and the new paganism of the Nazi extremists" (240).

The National Socialists had 30 articles planned for the day the traditional Christian faith was snuffed out, and replaced by Hitler's pagan vision for the nation. First of all, the Nazi government would control the church, which would be devoid of biblical Christianity. "The National Church is determined to exterminate irrevocably . . . the strange and foreign Christian faiths imported into Germany in the ill-omened year 800." (This was the year that Charlemagne was crowned the Christian emperor of the Holy Roman Empire, from which sprang the modern nation of Germany in the 19th century). The Bible would no longer be published or disseminated in Germany.

"The National Church will clear away from its altars all crucifixes, Bibles, and pictures of saints," replacing them with copies of Hitler's *Mein Kampf*, and a sword "to the left of the altar." Finally, the plan was to remove the "Christian crosses from all churches, cathedrals and chapels . . . and it must be superseded by the only unconquerable symbol, the swastika" (Shirer 240).

Hitler was no champion of Christianity. His religion was in stark contrast to everything about biblical Christianity. Why this libel that Adolf Hitler was somehow a Christian ever originated and is still parroted today, even among supposedly educated individuals, is mystifying. It is yet another demonstration of how history, either willfully, or through ignorance, can be so grossly misrepresented in the face of a mountain of actual facts.

LIBEL #11

FAKE JEWS CREATED ISRAEL BY STEALING THE LAND

"Tell them to get the Hell out of Palestine," responded the famous correspondent Helen Thomas to a question as to what the Jews of Israel should do. When then asked where they should then go, Thomas suggested Poland or Germany as to locations that were "home" to the Jews. Referring to the Arab population of "Palestine," Thomas said, "Remember. These people are occupied. It's their land." Later, she told Joy Behar, "Jews don't have a right to take other people's land."

When asked if her comments were anti-Semitic, Thomas retorted, "They're not Semites. Most of them are from Europe" (www.huffington post.com).

Thomas' harsh assessment is a good summary of the widespread contention that fake Jews from Europe created the modern nation of Israel by simply driving peace-loving Arabs out of their homes.

In the short film, "Christian Zionism: the Tragedy and the Turning," Charles E. Carlson charged that the Zionist movement (the desire of Jews to create a nation in Palestine), has been driven by a theological interpretation of Scripture (premillennialism) which he contended is a flawed interpretation of only recent vintage. Premillennialism is the belief that Jesus Christ will return to the earth, and set up a literal, one thousand year reign upon the earth, and that Israel will be restored as a nation. This view is opposed by the amillennial position, which hold the thousand year reign of Christ mentioned in the biblical Book of Revelation is only figurative, and the biblical prophecies found in the Old and New Testaments of a literal restoration of the nation of Israel in the land promised to Abraham and his descendants is fulfilled spiritually in the Christian church.

Carlson does not express a very high view of Scripture, dismissing the New Testament as full of "repetitious" stories. There are many devout, Bible-believing Christians on both sides of this debate on biblical prophecy, but Carlson's reasons for opposition to the premillennial position seem clear enough. He asserts that the premillennial interpretation leads to aggression against Islam, and is the principal cause of America's bad relations with many Islamic nations in the region. In one part of the film, Carlson said he could remember listening to bombs going off in Gaza, and thinking, "Imagine the United States is paying for all of this" (Carlson).

Not only does the film accuse premillennialist Christians of being taken in by the famous Scofield Reference Bible (edited by the late Cyrus Scofield), contending it was published by a "Zionist press" (Oxford Press) in 1908 for the purpose of creating Christian support for the restoration of Israel, he said that American Zionists were even responsible for getting President Woodrow Wilson into the first World War, because that would precipitate the creation of the nation of Israel.

The history of the Jews over the centuries has been one of horrific persecutions. As a political and military power, Israel reached its zenith under King David and his son King Solomon about one thousand years before the birth of Christ. After the death of Solomon, however, the nation divided into the nation of Israel to the north, and the nation of Judah to the south. In the 8th century, B.C., Assyria conquered the northern kingdom of Israel, and it disappeared from history. About 150 years later, the neo-Babylonian Empire conquered the southern kingdom of Judah, taking most of its inhabitants east to what is now Iraq. Less than 100 years later, after the Persians had now conquered the Babylonians, King Cyrus the Great of Persia issued an edict to allow the rebuilding of the Jewish temple in Jerusalem, and a later king, Artaxerxes, even allowed the Jews to rebuild the walls of the city.

Despite many Jews (so called because of the tribe of Judah, which dominated the southern kingdom) moving back to what they believed was the land which had been promised to them by God, many other Jews opted to remain in Babylon. When one mentions the Jewish *diaspora* (or dispersion), it was an event that happened more than once, and into more than one location. One should recall that Mary and Joseph fled with the infant Jesus from King Herod into Egypt, where a thriving Jewish community existed, even before the Jews' losing war against the Roman Empire led to the destruction of the second Jewish temple. This caused a mass scattering of the Jewish population, and some Jews continued to live in what is now Iraq and what is now Egypt until recent times.

This leads to one of the persistent myths surrounding the whole question of the creation of the state of Israel in 1948. Among those who argue the Jews in Palestine should just "go home," are those who contend that the Jews lived in a harmonious relationship with Arabs in Egypt, Iraq, and in other Islamic states of the Middle East before the Zionist movement. This assertion is wrong in several ways, one being the presumption that no Jews lived in Palestine before the Zionist movement gained momentum in the 19th century. A second error is the contention that Jews and Arabs lived in harmony, which is not the case. A third libel is that the Jews who entered Palestine and established the modern nation of Israel were virtually all from Europe. Closely related to this fabrication is that these European Jews had no ethnic relationship to the Jews of Bible times, but were rather descendants of a white European tribe known as the Khazars. Finally, of course, is the most serious libel, being that these "fake" Jews simply invaded the Holy Land, and uprooted indigenous Arabs (dubbed "Palestinians") who had been living in the land for centuries.

The theological dispute within Christianity over whether to interpret biblical prophecy under the premillennial or the amillennial umbrella is outside of the scope of this study. The other issues can be examined without taking a side in that dispute, upon which good Christian scholars do differ.

The assertion that the Jewish migration into Palestine was unnecessary because they were living in blissful harmony in Arab lands is simply false. King Faisel told Henry Kissinger in November, 1973, "Before the Jewish state was established, there existed nothing to harm good relations between Arabs and Jews." PLO leader Yassir Arafat expressed similar sentiments, claiming that Muslims, Jews, and Christians had been living in "peace and fraternity" for several centuries (Peters 33).

The reality is that the original relationship between Jews and Arabs *was* mostly harmonious, with some Arabs converting to Judaism. That changed radically with Muhammad and the rise of the Islamic religion. After he failed to win the Jews over to Islam, various restrictions were placed upon Jewish religious practices, they were forced to pay a special tax, and a Jew's testimony was held of no standing in any dispute with a Muslim (Peters 33-34).

And this persecution was not limited to the Middle Ages. In the 1950s, Anwar Sadat, then a leading minister for Gamal Nasser in Egypt, published an open letter to Adolf Hitler, hoping the German dictator was still living, and expressing sympathy for his efforts to exterminate the Jews. Egyptian writer Anis Mansour wrote in 1973, "People all over the world have come to realize that Hitler was right . . . would that he had finished it" (Peters 37).

Yemen law said that fatherless Jews under 13 could be taken from their mothers and raised as Muslims. Jews were actually stoned in Yemen at the time of the 1948 exodus. In 1912, over 2000 Jews in Yemen were disemboweled at Jaffa. On the eve of the 1948 Israeli declaration of independence, 82 Jews were murdered in a December, 1947, pogrom. One hundred and six of 170 Jewish shops were robbed bare, and four synagogues were burned to the ground, along with 220 Jewish homes (Peters 38-43).

In Iraq, about 123,000 Jews left Iraq between 1949 and 1952. The Jews had been in the country since the Babylonian Captivity, which was 1200 years before the Muslims conquered the country in A.D. 634. In 1941, the Iraqi Minister of Justice declared Judaism a "threat to mankind." Jews were forbidden to leave, however, with "Zionism," as it was called, considered a *capital* crime (Peters 43-45).

Similar stories can be told of the intense persecution in Egypt. One caliph in Egypt required Jews to wear miniature gold calf images around their necks, recalling the biblical story of when the Hebrews had turned to idolatry beneath Mount Sinai after God had brought them out of land of Egypt. In 1948, in only a seven-day period, 150 Jews were murdered or seriously wounded. In 1964, Nasser said that his sympathy was "with the Germans" in what they did to the Jews (Peters 46-49).

And on it goes, in Morocco, Algeria, and in Tunisia. Algeria denied citizenship to Jews. In Tunisia, they had no freedom, paid a heavy tax, and were forced to wear special clothes under the penalty of stoning. In Syria, the Great Synagogue of Aleppo was desecrated in 1945. Then, in December, 1947, most synagogues were burned, 150 Jewish homes were burned, along with five Jewish schools, and 50 shops. Police even assisted in the burning of an ancient manuscript of the Old Testament! A bombing of a synagogue in Damascus left over 20 dead (Peters 56-65).

In 1840, Jews in Syria were accused of murdering a priest and a servant, and using their blood in the Passover ceremony. This "blood libel," as it was called, is still repeated as the truth in Arab literature (Peters 65).

It was no better in Libya. Babies were beaten to death with iron bars and old men were hacked to pieces. More than 130 Jews were murdered in November, 1947 (Peters 69-70).

Of more than 850,000 Jews in Arab lands before Israel's statehood declaration, practically none remain today (Peters 116).

Perhaps these stories, only a fraction of the total, helps explain *why* Jews did not believe they were living in "harmony" in Arab lands. Zionism, the desire of the Jews to return from the diaspora back to their biblical homeland in modern-day "Palestine," existed a millennium *before* for Jews suffering in Arab lands. It was *not* the creation of Theodor Herzl, who called for a Jewish state in 1896. Wealthy Jewish banking families in Europe financed the development of settlements in Palestine.

The persecution of the Jews was not confined to just those living in the hostile lands of the Middle East, and it was not perpetrated only by Arab Muslims. Jews had contended with violent hostility in Europe, as well, even in its "Christian" culture. In Medieval Europe, the Jews were looked upon with suspicion, largely because they just did not "fit in" there any better than the unfortunate Jews who remained in the Arab lands of the Middle East. Their diet was considered odd. The Jews called pork, the principal meat of Europe, to be "unclean." Jews tended to keep to themselves (as though they had any other real choice), practiced a different religion, and carried the stigma that it was the Jews who had killed the Christ. The biblical story of the Jewish rejection of the Messiah was told over and over, with the words, "Let his blood be on us, and upon our children," taken as a prophecy by some that they were called upon to fulfill. Because they were often involved in money changing, many cited Jesus driving the money changers out of the temple. Many Jews, being involved in commercial enterprises like money changing and jewelry were often wealthier. Sadly, many just do not like the rich, which is still found in modern society. Coveting was not just a sin in biblical days.

When the bubonic plague wiped out perhaps as much as half the population of Europe in the 14th century, some desperate people seeking an answer decided the Jews were somehow responsible. Perhaps they were poisoning the drinking wells of Christians, it was conjectured. This led to a bonfire in Strasbourg, where thousands of Jews perished.

The Renaissance, the Reformation, and the Enlightenment brought huge changes to Europe, but nothing seemed to stop the persecution of the Jews. Hermann Ahlwardt, a member of the German Reichstag in the 19th century, refused to even consider Jews who converted to Christianity as acceptable. To him, Jewishness was not just a religion, but a race. "The Jew is no German," Ahlwardt said to the German Parliament. "A Jew who is born in Germany does not thereby become a German; he is still a Jew." Ahlwardt argued that it was "impossible" for Jews and Germans to live under the same laws in the same land (Spielvogel 84).

Anti-Jewish persecution was certainly not unique to Europe in Germany. It was common throughout Europe. Seventy-two percent of the entire Jewish population of the world lived in eastern Europe at the time. Organized massacres (pogroms) occurred periodically. Between 1903 and 1906, nearly 700 Russian towns and villages experienced pogroms. Hundreds of thousands of Jews chose to emigrate. Many Jews went to the United States, but thousands of others opted to move to their historic and biblical homeland in the Middle East (Spielvogel 849).

When European Jews chose to leave their homes in Europe, and move into a part of Palestine, many Jews were already living there. In fact, many Jewish families had never left, even after the Roman destruction of Jerusalem in A.D. 70.

In the centuries following the Arab conquest, Palestine was sparsely populated. In the 18th century, Thomas Shaw, a British archaeologist, noted that Palestine was "lacking in people to till its fertile soil" (Katz 1). Many of the historical and biblical cities were now little more than villages in the centuries before the beginning of the Jewish immigration into the land. Travelers from Europe in the early 1800s were surprised that they saw no boats on the Sea of Galilee. Exploring the land in 1867, American author Mark Twain lamented, "One may ride ten miles hereabouts and not see ten human beings." He described Palestine as "desolate" (Katz 5).

Many other tourists Europe expressed similar amazement that Palestine was largely unoccupied.

Dr. Carl Hermann Voss, chairman of the American Christian Palestine Committee, noted that it was the *Jewish* settlement that "restored the barren lands and drew it to the Arabs from neighboring countries" (Peters 245). This challenges another of the libels, perhaps the greatest, that Jews (with some refusing to admit that they are "real" Jews) came into Palestine, uprooted the "peace-loving" Palestinians, and created the modern nation-state of Israel.

When Jewish colonization began, in an organized fashion, in 1882, fewer than 150,000 Arabs lived in the land. Far from being the descendants of persons who had lived in Palestine for centuries, the vast majority of the Arab population are from immigrants and their descendants who moved into the land in the decades leading up to the establishment of modern Israel in 1948. Massive Jewish development of the land had been taking place for *decades* before 1917, certainly long before Herzl's Zionist movement (Peters 245).

Helen Thomas' suggestion that the Jews should go "home" to Germany and Poland is fantastic, considering that of the 8,861,800 Jews under National Socialist (Nazi) control, 5,933,900, or 67%, were murdered by the Nazis. It was not only Germany, but Austrians and Romanians also participated in this attempted extermination of Europe's Jews. Even many in France joined in the effort (Johnson 497).

Writing in *The History of the Jews*, historian Paul Johnson wrote that while the crime of the Holocaust was happening, "there was great resistance in America to accepting the fact of the Holocaust," even after American forces liberated the death camps. James Agee, writing in *The Nation*, refused to watch the atrocity films, denouncing them as just propaganda! Many American soldiers who saw the death camps were "furious" when many in the United States refused to believe that the Holocaust had really happened (Johnson 504).

Johnson wrote that some Jews expected that once the "extent" of Hitler's Final Solution became known, "an outraged humanity" would respond by demanding "this is enough." It was the Holocaust and world's mixed reaction to it, that gave the final push for Zionism to be fulfilled with a Jewish homeland in the Middle East. "The overwhelming lesson the Jews learned from the Holocaust was the imperative need to secure for themselves a permanent, self-contained and above all sovereign refuge where if necessary the whole of world Jewry could find safety from its enemies. The First World War made the Zionist state possible. The Second World War made it essential," Johnson wrote (517).

The British support for a Jewish homeland had changed since the Balfour Declaration of 1917. With the 1939 White Paper, the British took a different view of the Middle East, largely because of their need for Middle Eastern oil. Now, the British government did not want Jewish immigration into Palestine to anger the Arab world, and turn the Arabs against the British. This led some within the Zionist movement to resort to terrorist tactics. A future Israeli prime minister, Menachem Begin, blew up the King David Hotel, killing 28 British citizens, 41 Arabs, 17 Jews, and five others, in an effort to force the British to abandon their holdings in the Middle East. (The British had been given a "mandate" by the League of Nations over what is called Palestine). Begin insisted that an advance warning had been given, but such terror tactics, so common in recent years, were even more shocking at the time. The British had been reluctant to leave the area, fearing a resultant slaughter of the Jews, but after such terrorist acts, they decided it was time to leave the Jews to their fate (Johnson 523).

In 1946, Transjordan, part of the British Mandate, became the *Arab* Palestinian state, two years before the creation of the Jewish homeland in Israel. The Jews took only a small portion of Palestine, less than 8,000 square miles, compared to 38,000 square miles for Transjordan. Yet, today, many commentators, either from ignorance or malevolence, assert that Palestine and Israel are the same. From the time of new Jewish settlements in the 1870s, until 1948 and Israeli statehood, the area of Jewish settlement changed little.

Although President Harry Truman pushed for the creation of a Jewish state, American and British oil companies opposed him. Soviet dictator Joseph Stalin also supported the creation of the state of Israel, expecting it to be socialist, hoping to reduce British influence in the region. The communist government of Czechoslovakia even sold weapons to Israel (Johnson 525-526).

Interestingly, the independence of Israel, declared on May 14, 1948, occurred within a narrow window of opportunity. Within a year, both the United States and the Soviet Union would most likely have opposed its creation. Those who take a certain theological stance on the modern nation of Israel would no doubt chalk this up to the intervention of Divine Providence (Johnson 526).

As soon as the United Nations partition vote was taken, Azzam Pasha, then secretary general of the Arab League, went on radio and declared the Arab world would exterminate the Jews. By March, 1948, over 1200 Jews had been killed in terrorist acts. The night that Israeli leader David Ben-Gurion announced the nation's independence, Egyptian air raids began. In the months leading up to the first Arab-Israeli War, the war, and in its aftermath, an estimated 656,000 Arabs fled Palestine. During the years leading up to the first war, more than one-half million Jews living in Arab lands in 1945, also fled, mostly to Israel (Johnson 526-528).

The Israeli government systematically resettled all its refugees, as a matter of policy, while the Arab governments insisted that Arab refugees remain in "temporary" camps, awaiting the day the Jews would be driven from Palestine. Abba Eban explained the Jewish partition strategy. "(W)e relied on the general premise of a historical connection . . . Since Hebron was full of Arabs, we did not ask for it. Since Beersheba was virtually empty, we put in a successful claim. The central Zionist thesis was there existed sufficient room with Eretz Israel for a densely populated Jewish society to be established without displacing Arab populations" (Johnson 529; 531).

In 1949, the Israeli government offered to negotiate, but the Arabs refused, insisting that the Israelis retire behind the 1947 UN partition lines (which the Arabs had previously rejected) without Arab recognition of the state of Israel. In its first seven years of existence, over 1300 Israelis were murdered during Arab raids. Wars in 1956, 1967, and 1973 failed to drive the Jews "into the sea," as multiple Arab leaders vowed to do, but these wars *did* lead to Israel gaining even more land, including the control of all Jerusalem, and the Sinai Peninsula, which provided a buffer in case the Egyptians attacked again (Johnson 532).

Hope of a general peace settlement in the Middle East brightened, when, in 1978, Egyptian President Anwar Sadat (the same man who had once written that Hitler was on the right track) opted to cut a deal, the Camp David Treaty, with Israeli Prime Minister Menachem Begin (who himself had committed the terrorist attack on the King David Hotel). Other Arab nations, however, reacted with fury against Egypt, and President Sadat. Just a few years later, Arab terrorists assassinated Sadat for daring to make peace with Israel.

It is clear to anyone who examines the historical record that the Jews did not simply expel Palestinians from their homes, but that Jews from neighboring Arab countries and from Europe moved into the region, which was mostly unoccupied and desolate, in an effort to escape centuries of persecutions, culminating in the Holocaust of World War II. Yet, another libel of more recent vintage used in the arsenal of propaganda weapons used against the nation of Israel is that these Jews really are not even the Jews we read about in the Bible. According to this theory, Israel was established by "fake" Jews from Europe, who are not biological descendants from the Jews of antiquity. This ignores the thousands of Jews who fled from horrific Arab persecution in the Middle East, and the smaller numbers of Jews who were already residing in their ancient land.

The basis of this idea that the Israeli Jews are not real Jews, but rather "fake" Jews of European blood, is that the European Jews were actually descendants of the Khazars of Khazaria, a people found in the area from the Volga steppes to eastern Crimea and the northern Caucasas. Khazaria was a vibrant trading region, which served as an excellent "buffer zone" between the expansionist Muslims of the Middle East and the Christian Byzantine Empire.

The Khazar state was eventually destroyed by the Kievan Rus ruler Sviatoslave I, between 965 and 969.

Before that happened, however, Khazar royalty and much of the aristocracy converted to Judaism, while much of the general population remained pagan, Christian, or Muslim, along with a good-sized number of Jewish converts. The Khazars responded to the Islamic invasions of the 7th century with some military actions of their own, and the two sides fought fiercely until the demise of the Khazars in the 10th century.

Because the Khazars were the *only* Jewish state to rise between the fall of the Second Temple in the Roman-Jewish War of A.D. 66-70, and the establishment of modern Israel in 1948, we now have a widely-held belief that the Ashkenazi Jews are largely the descendants of these Khazars. It should be noted, of course, even the great King David himself was descended from some non-Jews (e.g. Ruth and Rahab), as is Jesus Himself. Throughout history, many individuals were attracted to the Jewish faith, and were recognized as fully Jewish upon conversion. It is possible that the largest addition to the Semitic base of the modern Jew was from the Khazars, but if so, it is still only a tiny addition. According to Harry Ostrer, in *Legacy: A Genetic History of the Jewish People*, novelist Arthur Koestler published a book in 1976, *The Thirteenth Tribe*, in which he advanced the thesis that Ashkenazi, or eastern European Jews, were mostly descended from the Khazars, rather than the "Israelites of antiquity" (Ostrer 26-27).

This challenged the prevailing view that most of the Ashkenazi Jews were descendants of Semitic Middle Eastern Jews who moved into Europe through Italy and the Rhineland. Koestler argued instead they were Khazars who had moved into Russia, Ukraine, and Poland. Koestler mistakenly believed that this would "defuse" anti-Semitism. If the European Jews were *not* descended from the biblical Jews, they could not then be blamed for the crucifixion of Christ. As Ostrer commented, "Ironically, Koestler's thesis gained currency with anti-Semitic groups who believed that identifying most Jews as non-Semitic would seriously undermine their historical claims to the land of Israel" (Ostrer 26-27).

Ostrer is a medical doctor and a professor of pathology and genetics at Albert Einstein College of Medicine and Director of Genetic and Genomic Testing at Montefiore Medical Center. Using the studies of others, combined with his own, Ostrer demonstrates that the Jews from the various groups of the Jewish diaspora *are* linked by genetics and biology.

Dr. Ostrer's book is a powerful work of scholarship, and he examines the question of common Jewish ethnicity from multiple angles. He notes that the Roman Emperor Titus brought many Jews to Rome following the Roman-Jewish War, which resulted in the destruction of the Jewish Temple in Jerusalem in A.D. 70. Spanish Jews migrated to Rome to escape the Inquisition, where those "Sephardic" Jews "co-mingled" with the "Roman" Jews. Because Roman Jews had a low frequency of disease mutations that were found in both Ashkenazi and Sephardic populations, he speculated that they were the principal ancestors of the Ashkenazi Jews (Ostrer 145).

In his book, *DNA & Tradition: The Genetic Link to the Ancient Hebrews*, Yaakov Kleiman wrote, "Haplotypes have also helped the identity seekers to retrace the path of the wandering Ashkenazi Jew. We who hail from East Europe most likely migrated there from Alsace and Rhineland, as confirmed by Yiddish, a form of Low German." Ostrer concluded from his study of Roman Jews that the Ashkenazi lived in Italy for a thousand years before they migrated into Alsace and Rhineland. "There's no genetic difference between Ashkenazic and Roman Jews, who say they have lived in Italy for 2,000 years," he observed (Kleiman 95).

The Roman historian Seutonius wrote that in the middle of the First Century, the Emperor Claudius expelled the Jews from Rome because they "constantly made disturbances at the instigation of Chrestus." Historians believe this a reference to the dispute between Jews and Christians concerning whether Jesus was the Christ, or Jewish Messiah, and that the Romans did not yet fully differentiate between the Jews and the Christians. This expulsion of the Jews from Rome is also mentioned in the New Testament (Acts 18:2).

In his study of the Cohanim (popularly called Cohen), Ostrer said that this group had very little intermarriage with non-Jews, even proselytes, and yet they differ little with the rest of the Jews. "In ancient times," Ostrer wrote, "the Cohanim officiated in the Temple" (Ostrer 87).

Despite his remarkable findings of a blood relationship between all the various branches of Jewry (including Sephardic and Ashkenazi), he did find some genetic ties with Ukrainians, Russians, and Central Asian populations. He believes this may very well be the traces of the Khazars with Ashkenazi Jews, but it might also simply be more of a relationship with Ukrainians, Polish, and Russian peoples. The Ashkenazi Jews proved to be genetically distinct from the Turkic peoples of Central Asia, which are people thought to have descended from the Khazars. Ostrer contended that this "tended to negate" Koestler's concept of a Khazarian origin for Ashkenazi, from the book, *The Thirteenth Tribe* (Ostrer 94, 127, 149).

Ostrer's conclusions, based on the evidence that can be found discussed at great length in his book, each of the various Jewish ethnic groups "demonstrated Semitic ancestry and had variable degrees of admixture with European population." In short, Ostrer's studies indicate that the Jews who have migrated into Palestine, whether of Middle Eastern or European stock, have a common Semitic origin, going back to the same Middle Eastern Jews we read about in the Bible, with some limited admixture with the Khazars and others (Ostrer 148).

Kleiman wrote that the genetic research "indicates that despite physical separation and nearly 2,000 years, both the Ashkenazic and Sephardic Jewish communities maintain a Y-Chromosome profile largely derived from the Middle East." Ostrer estimated that the European admixture, from conversion or intermarriage, over 80 generations is an extremely low 0.5% per generation (Kleiman 95).

Summarizing Ostrer's and Kleiman's findings, the general Ashkenazi paternal gene pool does not appear to be similar to that of present-day Turkish speakers. This argues against the suggestion that most Ashkenazi are descended from the Khazars. However, the Khazar case is far from closed. Recent studies have found an unusual haplotype, not found in the Middle East in high percentage in the Ashkenazi Levites, leading to speculation that this may possibly be of Khazar origin. The majority of the Ashkenazi population have a similar male genetic lineage profile to Roman Jews and to most Sephardic groups as well. The genetic research confirms that most Jews today are indeed the descendants of ancestors who came from the Middle East (Kleiman 95; Ostrer 92, 94, 104, 126, 127, 145, 148).

In the end, one has to ask what I believe to be a most obvious question. Even if one were to concede that the Jews of Europe were *not* descended from Abraham, but rather were of European origin, they are still Jews. All through Jewish history, there have been converts to the Jewish religion, including members of the family tree of King David, and Jesus Christ (at least on His mother's side), and no one can make a serious argument that David and Jesus were not real Jews! The European persecutors of the Jews, including Hitler, certainly did not regard the Jews in Germany as of European ancestry.

Adolf Hitler's teen-age friend, August Kubizek, recalled that one day as they were walking around their home town, the adolescent Hitler pointed at a Jewish synagogue in Linz, Austria, and told Kubizek that that building "doesn't belong in Linz" (Kubizek 94). Later, Hitler himself recalled in his book, *Mein Kampf*, that while he was walking in Vienna, he encountered what he believed to be a strange man with a long black coat and side whiskers.

"Is this a Jew?" was Hitler's first thought, "But the longer I stared at this foreign face, the more my question assumed a new form: 'Is this a German?'" (Shirer 20).

As Hitler rose to power in Germany, his anti-Jewish tirades were not considered all that unusual to the Jews in Germany. After all, they had experienced such vicious anti-Semitic prejudice for centuries.

So, who can blame the Jews of Europe for wanting to go to a homeland in Palestine, to the land that God had given to Abraham *and his descendants*? And, as we have seen, the persecution had been almost unrelenting not only in Europe, but also in the Arab lands of the Middle East.

The Jews did not "steal" the land in Palestine from the Arabs. As Mark Twain said, the land was "desolate" before the arrival of the Jews, not only from Europe, but also from neighboring lands in the Middle East, from which the Jews also desired to escape an almost continual nightmare of persecution.

To say the Jews of Israel are not really Jews, and they simply stole Palestine from peace-loving Arabs already living there, certainly must rank as one of history's greatest libels.

TO THE JURY

I n an actual court case, libel must be proved by "clear and convincing evidence," which is a higher standard than the usual "by preponderance of the evidence," which is found in most civil cases. It is a standard similar to "beyond reasonable doubt," which one finds with a criminal case.

I hope that I have accomplished a defense of the people found in each of the chapters of this book. A defense from unfair and untrue accusations. In none of the cases have I attempted to argue that any of the individuals (such as Marie Antoinette) or the groups (such as the Jews in Israel) are *perfect*. My goal is much more modest. I hoped to defend each from some specific charge, or a narrow range of charges. Because of this, these chapters are not intended as biographies. Others have already written those, and I would encourage the reader to consider some of the books and articles in the bibliography for additional information, if it is so desired.

What I have tried to do with this book is to provide the reader with an overview of the issues involved in each of the historical libels I have alleged, and put these stories all in one place. I have faced frustration over the years in hearing statements made that I believe are untrue, some falsehood told about some historical person, who can no longer defend himself. The only chapter concerning someone who is still alive is the one on Justice Clarence Thomas.

The closest that I came to a general biography is the chapter dealing with Marie Antoinette. While still not a standard biography, I felt it necessary to give more coverage to her life, because her whole life has been unfairly maligned in the popular culture. For example, one time I was discussing some of the personalities in history whom I contend have been unfairly treated by "history," and mentioned that Marie Antoinette never uttered those infamous words, "Let them eat cake!" One man responded, "But it did express her attitude." Actually, I hope that I have demonstrated that it really did *not* express her attitude.

My chapter on Thomas Jefferson was only intended to defend him from one specific ugly accusation that he fathered children by his slave. It is the very type of charge that far too many simply wish to believe. Others have heard some vague statement that "DNA studies" have provided proof that Jefferson *was* the father of children by Sally Hemings. It is not my purpose to defend Jefferson for anything else, which would be the subject of another chapter or article, if I so chose to defend him on some other particular accusation.

This illustrates, though, how many of these libels get started and persist in the public mind. The results of the DNA testing were twisted to provide President Bill Clinton some defense when he was entangled in a sex scandal. The argument seems to be that if *Thomas Jefferson* did such a despicable thing, perhaps Clinton should get a "pass" for something much less odious. It is a stark example of how the reputation of one of our greatest of founding fathers is so willingly shredded to provide cover so as to advance a liberal political or social cause in the present. After an avalanche of publicity for the DNA tests, falsely reported, even those who do not share the goal of those who perpetrated the "libel" are convinced as well. They understandably do not know there is more to the story than what has been presented by the media.

Those who take a more progressive or "liberal" view of modern politics learned a long time ago that winning the story of the past is the key to capturing the present, and with it, our future. While conservatives usually go onto the next battle in the "culture war," if you will, liberals are simply not going to allow those on the political or cultural Right to ever win even one battle. To them the battle is never over until they have won it. Although it appeared at the time that conservatives had won the "battle" over Anita Hill's charges against Supreme Court Justice Clarence Thomas, those on the political Left went to work. With their "soldiers" in the media, the popular culture, and in academia, they began to rewrite the history of the Thomas-Hill contest, to fit the liberal viewpoint. While polls taken in the immediate aftermath of the events indicated that the general public believed Thomas over Hill, this unholy trinity (media, popular culture, academia) was permitted—-largely unimpeded by those on the

Right—-to simply change the narrative. Today, the conventional belief is that Thomas sexually harassed Hill.

While the struggle over Thomas' confirmation was a little over 20 years ago, and is very recent "history," it is little different from the motive behind the other libels discussed in this book. It is an amazing thing that some of the same individuals who declare that George Washington was *not* a Christian will then argue that Adolf Hitler *was* a Christian. In both cases, the motive is to denigrate the Christian faith. Similarly, the chapter on William Jennings Bryan at the Scopes Monkey Trial is another example of how hated the Christian faith is in our modern world. Again, my defense of Bryan is *not* of the entirety of his political career (far too liberal for my tastes), just a defense of him in the unfair and inaccurate portrayal found in the movie, *Inherit the Wind*. In that movie, Bryan was pictured as some sort of buffoon, which he certainly was not. It is said that Hollywood created an image of the American West that never was, but always will be. Much of the same can be said of many other historical events that have been maliciously altered on the silver screen to advance the world view of the modern liberal.

I am under no illusions that this one book will, by itself, halt the parroting of the libels discussed in it. For one thing, many would not change their minds regardless of the evidence I presented. But some will. I especially want this book read by those whose minds are open to the facts.

It is my sincere hope that you will take the facts presented in this book, and share them to change others' minds. Just remember, we can only do what we can do. As Robert E. Lee told the Army of Northern Virginia, when some did not want to surrender in April, 1865, "You have done all your duty, leave the results to God."

I can assure you that you will, at some point, hear these libels repeated by a family members, a co-worker, or an acquaintance. Here is a concrete suggestion. When someone repeats the falsehood, "Joe McCarthy created the Hollywood Blacklist while Chairman of the House Committee on Un-American Activities," all you have to say is, "I read about that in a book (may I suggest you could say "great book" to really persuade them). The author, some guy who teaches college history, said that McCarthy, being a senator, was not even on *any* House committees. Furthermore, he was not interested in Communists in Hollywood, but rather the Communist spies who were employed in sensitive positions in the American government."

Above all, be polite. You want to win a convert, not just win an argument. If it is true, you might even say, "I used to think that, too, but this book, *History's Greatest Libels*, which I read recently explained what *really* happened." Then, you could suggest that they buy a copy, or even better, you could give them a copy!

And, think about it this way. If you were Christopher Columbus, James K. Polk, Warren Harding, or anyone of the many others written about in this book, who are no longer able to speak for themselves, wouldn't you want your historical reputation defended?

I would, too. That is why I was driven to write this book. It is time to counter-attack against those who have had this field to themselves, for far too long.

FOR ADDITIONAL DISCOUNTED COPIES OF *HISTORY'S GREATEST LIBELS*, please write Steve Byas, P.O. Box 724, Norman, Oklahoma, or call me at (405) 366-1125. Thank you for all of your support! Also, feel free to e-mail me your thoughts, at byassteve@yahoo.com.

I t is highly recommended for those with additional interest in the subjects raised in this book, to read the sources cited.

LIBEL #1 WASHINGTON WAS A DEIST, NOT A CHRISTIAN

Fitzpatrick, John C., Editor. *The Writings of George Washington, Volume XII.* Washington: U.S. Government Printing Office, 1932.

Gragg, Rod. *By the Hand of Providence.* New York: Howard Books, 2011.

Gottfried, Paul. *The American Conservative, http.//www.the americanconservative.com,* retrieved by author 8/15/2014.

Johnson, William J. *George Washington, the Christian.* Forgotten Books reprint, New York: Abingdon Press, 1919.

Sparks, Jared. *www.christiananswers.net,* retrieved by author, 8/28/2014.

LIBEL #2

THOMAS JEFFERSON HAD CHILDREN BY HIS SLAVE

Barton, David. *The Jefferson Lies.* Nashville: Thomas Nelson, 2012.

Bernstein, R.B. *Thomas Jefferson.* Oxford: Oxford University Press, 2003.

Brodie, Fawn. *Thomas Jefferson: An Intimate History.* New York: Norton, 1974.

Hyland, William G. *In Defense of Thomas Jefferson.* New York: Thomas Dunne, 2009.

Meachum, Jon. *Thomas Jefferson, The Art of Power.* New York: Random House, 2012.

LIBEL #3

JAMES POLK WENT TO WAR AGAINST MEXICO TO OBTAIN TEXAS

Faulk, Odie B., Editor. *The Mexican War, Changing Interpretations.* Chicago: Sage Books, 1973.

LIBEL #4 HARDING WAS OUR WORST PRESIDENT

Carson, Clarence. *The Growth of America, 1878-1928.* Greenville, Alabama: American Textbook Committee, 1985.

Daugherty, Harry M. *The Inside Story of the Harding Tragedy.* Belmont: Western Islands, 1975.

Dean, John W. *Warren G. Harding.* New York: Times Books, 2004.

Ferrell, Robert H. *The Strange Deaths of President Harding.* Columbia: University of Missouri Press, 1996.

Grant, James. *The Forgotten Depression, 1921: The Crash that Cured Itself.* New York: Simon & Schuster, Kindle Edition.

Hayward, Steven F. *Politically Incorrect Guide to the Presidents.* Washington: Regnery Publishing, 2012.

Stratton, David H. *Tempest over Teapot Dome: The Story of Albert B. Fall.* Norman: University of Oklahoma Press, 1998.

LIBEL #5

THE SCOPES TRIAL MADE A MONKEY OUT OF WILLIAM JENNINGS BRYAN

Cornelius, R.M. *Scopes: Creation on Trial.* Green Forest, Arkansas: Master Books, 1999.

Hunter, George. *Civic Biology.* Kindle Edition of 1914 edition.

Kazin, Michael. *A Godly Hero: The Life of William Jennings Bryan.* New York: Anchor Books, 2007.

Koening, Louis. *Bryan: A Political Biography of William Jennings Bryan.* New York: G.P. Putnam's Sons, 658.

Perloff, James. "Monkeying With the Facts," *The New American,* August 14, 2000, p. 14.

LIBEL #6 JOE McCARTHY SMEARED INNOCENT PEOPLE

Cohn, Roy. *McCarthy: The Answer to Tail-Gunner Joe.* New York: Manor Books, 1977.

Coulter, Ann. "Liberals' Secret Weapon: Conservatives Who Don't Read," *Human Events,* August 13, 2012, p. 15.

Evans, M. Stanton. "When Conservatives Parrot Liberal Lies about Joe McCarthy," *Human Events,* August 20, 2012, p. 22.

Evans, M. Stanton. *Blacklisted by History.* New York: Crown Publishing, 2007.

Evans, Medford. *The Assassination of Joe McCarthy.* Belmont, Massachusetts: Western Islands, 1970.

Flynn, John T. *McCarthy, His War on American Reds and the Story of Those Who Oppose Him.* Mountain City, Tennessee: Sacred Truth Publishing, 2009.

Grigg, William Norman. "McCarthy Targeted Again," *The New American,* June 16, 2003, p. 16.

Herman, Arthur. *Joseph McCarthy.* New York: The Free Press, 2000.

Rovere, Richard. *Senator Joe McCarthy.* Berkeley: University of California Press, 1959.

LIBEL #7 CLARENCE THOMAS SEXUALLY HARASSED ANITA HILL

Brock, David. *The Real Anita Hill.* New York: The Free Press, 1994.

Danforth, John C. *Resurrection, The Confirmation of Clarence Thomas.* New York: Viking, 1994.

Hill, Anita. *Speaking Truth to Power.* New York: Anchor Books, 1997.

Thomas, Andrew Peyton. *Clarence Thomas, a Biography.* San Francisco: Encounter Books, 2001.

Thomas, Clarence. *My Grandfather's Son.* New York: Harper Collins, 2007.

LIBEL #8 COLUMBUS WAS A MONSTER WHO DID NOTHING GOOD

Ardon, John. www.therealpresence.org/archives/Christopher_Columbus_003.htm

Delaney, Carol. *Columbus and the Quest for Jerusalem.* New York: The Free Press, 2011.

De Seno, Tommy. "The Truth About Columbus," www.foxnews.com/opinion/2010/2011/tommy-seno-columbus-day-franciscoba-badilla-native-americans.

Grant, George. *The Last Crusader.* Wheaton, Illinois: Crossway Books, 1992.

Morrison, Samuel Eliot. *Christopher Columbus, Mariner.* Boston: Mentor Book, 1942.

Schweikert, Larry. *48 Liberal Lies About American History.* New York: Sentinel, 2009.

LIBEL #9 MARIE ANTOINETTE WAS RESPONSIBLE FOR THE FRENCH REVOLUTION

http://www.marieantoinette.org

Fraser, Antonia. *Marie Antoinette, The Journey.* New York: Random House, Anchor Books Edition, 2002.

Quill, Carolly Erickson. *To the Scaffold: The Life of Marie Antoinette.* New York: William Morrow, 1999.

Thomas, Chantel. *The Wicked Queen: The Origins of the Myth of Marie-Antoinette.* New York: Zone Books, 1999.

Webster, Nesta H. *The French Revolution: A Study in Democracy.* Christian Book Club of America reprint, 1969.

LIBEL #10 HITLER WAS A CHAMPION OF CHRISTIANITY

Bullock, Alan. *Hitler: A Study in Tyranny.* New York: Harper Perennial Edition, 1991.

Fischer, Klaus. *Nazi Germany: A New History.* New York: Barnes & Noble, 1998.

Kershaw, Ian. *The Hitler Myth: Image and Reality in the Third Reich.* Oxford: Oxford University Press, 2001.

Kubizek, August, translated by Geoffrey Brooks. *The Young Hitler I Knew.* London: Greenhill Books, 1953, 2006 edition.

Shirer, William L. *The Rise and Fall of the Third Reich.* New York: Simon & Schuster, 1960.

Speer, Albert, translated by Richard and Clara Winston. *Inside the Third Reich: Memoirs.* New York: McMillan Publishing, 1970.

Toland, John. *Adolf Hitler.* New York: Ballantine Books, 1976.

Trevor-Roper, H.R. *Hitler's Table Talk.* Cameron & Stevens, Enigma Books, 2000.

LIBEL #11
FAKE JEWS CREATED ISRAEL BY STEALING THE LAND

Helen Thomas to Joy Bahar, www.huffingtonpost.com/helen-thomas-joy-baher-israel

Carlson, Charles E. "Christian Zionism: The Tragedy and the Turning." Retrieved from www.youtube.com

Katz, Joseph. "Palestine, a land virtually laid waste with little population." Eretz Yisroel.org.

Kleiman. *DNA &Tradition: A Genetic Link to the Ancient Hebrews.* Jerusalem: Devora Publishing, 2004.

Kubizek, August. Translated by Geoffrey Brooks. *The Young Hitler I Knew.* London: Greenhill Books, 1953, 2006 edition.

Johnson, Paul. *A History of the Jews.* New York: Harper Perennial, 1987.

Ostrer, Harry. *Legacy: A Genetic History of the Jewish People.* Oxford: Oxford University Press, 2012.

Peters, Joan. *From Time Immemorial: The Origins of the Arab-Jewish Conflict over Palestine.* Chicago: JKAP Publications, 2002.

Shirer, William L. *The Rise and Fall of Adolf Hitler.* New York: Scholastic Books Services, 1964.

Spielvogel, Jackson J. *Western Civilization.* Boston: Wadsworth, 2012.

CPSIA information can be obtained at www.ICGtesting.com
Printed in the USA
BVOW11s0728041115

425536BV00018B/265/P

9 781457 539671